The Holy Buddha-Christ Bible

Concise Italic Edition

Bodhisattva Fellowship

Library of Congress Control Number: 2007900760

ISBN: 978-0-9759039-0-2

Contents

The Holy Buddha-Christ Bible

Concise Italic Edition

The Words of Buddha and Christ are Italicized

The Dharma of the Buddha
(Circa 563 – 483 B.C.)

The Four Noble Truths
of Suffering

The Four Noble Truths of Suffering

The Blessed One said:

As long, disciples, as the absolutely true knowledge and insight in regards to the Four Noble Truths was not quite clear in me, so long was I not sure whether I had won to that Supreme Enlightenment which is unsurpassed in all the world with its heavenly beings, evil spirits, ascetics and priests, and men. But as soon as the absolutely true knowledge and insight in regards to these Four Noble Truths had become perfectly clear in me, there arose in me the assurance that I had won to that Supreme Enlightenment unsurpassed.

And I discovered that profound truth, so difficult to perceive, difficult to understand, tranquilizing and sublime, which is not to be gained by mere reasoning and is visible only to the wise.

The world, however, is given to pleasure, delighted with pleasure, enchanted with pleasure. Verily, worldly beings will hardly understand the Law of Conditionality, the Dependent Origination of all things.

Incomprehensible to them also will be the end of all formations, the forsaking of every substratum of rebirth, the fading away of craving, detachment, extinction, Nirvana.

Yet, there are those whose eyes are only a little covered with dust: They will understand the Truth.

The Dharma of the Buddha

The First Truth
The Noble Truth of Suffering

What now is the Noble Truth of Suffering?
Birth is suffering, Decay is suffering, Death is suffering,
Sorrow, Lamentation, Pain, Grief and Despair are suf-
fering, not to get what one desires is suffering. In short,
the Five Aggregates of Existence are suffering. And
what, in brief, are the Five Aggregates of Existence
connected with cleaving? They are the Bodily Form,
Feeling, Perception, Mental Formations and States of
Consciousness.

All formations are transient and all formations are
subject to suffering. All things are without an Ego-
entity. Form is transient, feeling is transient, perception
is transient, mental formations are transient and con-
sciousness is transient. And of that which is subject to
suffering and change, one cannot rightly say, 'This I
am. This is my Ego.'

Suppose a man, who can see, were to behold the
many bubbles on the Ganges River as they were float-
ing along. And he watches them and examines them
carefully. After carefully examining them, they appear
to him as empty, unreal and without substance. In
exactly the same way does the disciple behold all the

The Four Noble Truths of Suffering

bodily forms, feelings, perceptions, mental formations and states of consciousness, whether they be of the past, or of the present, or of the future, far or near. And he watches them and examines them carefully, and, after carefully examining them, they appear to him as empty, void and without an Ego.

Whoever delights in bodily form, or feeling, or perception, or mental formations or states of consciousness delights in suffering. And whoever delights in suffering will not be freed from suffering. Thus I say.

Inconceivable is the beginning of this Samsara, not to be discovered at first by beings, who, obstructed by ignorance and ensnared by craving, are hurrying and hastening through this round of rebirths.

Which do you think is more: the flood of tears, which weeping and wailing you have shed upon this long way, hurrying and hastening through this round of rebirths, united to the undesired, separated from the desired, this or the waters of the four oceans? For a long time you have suffered the death of father and mother, sons, daughters, sisters and brothers. And while you were suffering, you have verily shed more tears upon this long way than there is water in the four oceans.

Which do you think is more: the stream of blood that, through your being beheaded, has flowed upon

*this long way, or the waters of the four oceans? For a
long time you have been caught as highway robbers or
adulterers, and through your being beheaded verily
more blood has flowed upon this long way than there
is water in the four oceans.*

*But how is this possible? Inconceivable is the begin-
ning of this Samsara, not to be discovered at first by
beings, who, obstructed by ignorance and ensnared by
craving, are hurrying and hastening through this round
of rebirths. And thus have you undergone suffering,
undergone torment, undergone misfortune and filled
the graveyards full. Verily, long enough to be dissatis-
fied with every form of existence, long enough to turn
away and free yourselves from them all!*

The Second Truth
The Noble Truth of the Origin of Suffering

*What now is the Noble Truth of the Origin of
Suffering? It is the craving which gives rise to fresh re-
birth and bound up with pleasure and lust, now here,
now there, seeks ever-fresh delight. There is the Sensual
Craving, the Craving for Eternal Existence and the
Craving for Temporal Happiness.*

But where do these cravings arise and take root?

The Four Noble Truths of Suffering

*Wherever in the world there are delightful and pleas-
urable things, there these cravings arise and take root.
Forms, sounds, smells, bodily touches and ideas are
delightful and pleasurable, and there these cravings
arise and take root. If, namely, when perceiving a
visible form, a sound, odor, taste, bodily contact or
an idea in the mind, if the object is pleasant, one is
attracted, and if unpleasant, one is repelled. Thus,
whatever kind of feeling one experiences - pleasant,
unpleasant or indifferent - one approves of and cherishes the feeling and clings to it. And while doing so,
lust springs up. But lust for feelings means clinging to
existence. On clinging to existence depends the Process
of Becoming, on the Process of Becoming depends
future birth and dependent on birth are decay and
death, sorrow, lamentation, pain, grief and despair.
Thus arises this whole mass of suffering. This is called
the Noble Truth of the Origin of Suffering.*

*Verily, due to sensual craving, conditioned through
sensual craving, impelled by sensual craving, entirely
moved by sensual craving, kings fight with kings,
princes with princes, citizens with citizens, the mother
quarrels with the son, the son with the mother, the
father with the son, the son with the father, brother
with sister, sister with brother, friend with friend.*

The Dharma of the Buddha

*Thus given to dissention, quarreling and fighting,
they fall upon each other with fists, sticks or weapons.
And thereby they suffer death or deadly pain.*

*And further, due to sensual craving, conditioned
through sensual craving, impelled by sensual craving,
entirely moved by sensual craving, people break into
houses, rob and plunder, pillage entire villages, commit
highway robbery and seduce the wives of others. Then
the rulers have such people caught and inflict on them
various forms of punishment. Thereby, they incur death
or deadly pain. Now, this is the misery of sensual craving, the heaping up of suffering in this present life due
to sensual craving and entirely dependent on sensual
craving.*

*And further, people take the evil way in deeds, the
evil way in words, and the evil way in thoughts. And
by taking the evil way in deeds, words and thoughts, at
the dissolution of the body, after death, they fall into a
downward state of existence, a state of suffering, into
perdition and the abyss of hell.*

*For the owners of their deeds are the heirs of their
deeds, their deeds are the womb from which they
sprang, with their deeds they are bound up; their deeds
are their refuge. Whatever deeds they do, whether good
or evil, of such they will be the heirs. And wherever*

such beings spring into existence, there their deeds will ripen, there they will earn the fruits of those deeds, be it in this life, or be it in the next life, or be it in any other future life.

There will come a time when the mighty oceans will dry up, vanish and be no more. There will come a time when the mighty earth will be devoured by fire, perish and be no more. Yet, there will be no end to the suffering of beings, who, obstructed by ignorance and ensnared by craving, are hurrying and hastening through this round of rebirths.

The Third Truth
The Noble Truth of the Extinction of Suffering

What now is the Noble Truth of the Extinction of Suffering? It is the complete fading away and extinction of craving, its forsaking and giving up, the liberation and detachment from it.

Where may craving vanish? Where may craving be extinguished? Wherever in the world there are delightful and pleasurable things, there craving may vanish, there it may be extinguished. Be it in the past, present or future, whoever regards the delightful and pleasurable things in this world as impermanent, miserable and without an Ego, as a disease and sorrow, it is they who overcome craving.

And released from Sensual Craving, released from the Craving for Eternal Existence, they do not return, do not enter again into worldly existence. This, truly, is the Peace, this is the Highest, namely the end of all formations, the forsaking of every substratum of re-birth, the fading away of craving, detachment, extinction, Nirvana.

Enraptured with lust, enraged with anger, blinded by delusion, overwhelmed with mind ensnared, man aims at his own ruin, at the ruin of others, at the ruin of both parties, and he experiences mental pain and grief. But if lust, anger and delusion are given up man aims neither at his own ruin, nor at the other's ruin, nor at the ruin of both parties, and he experiences no mental pain and grief.

This is Nirvana immediate, visible in this life, inviting, attractive and comprehensible to the wise. And for a disciple thus freed, in whose heart dwells peace, there is nothing to be added to what has been done, and nothing more remains for him to do. Just as a rock of one solid mass remains unshaken by the wind, even so, neither forms, nor sounds, nor odors, nor tastes, nor contacts of any kind, neither the desired nor the undesired can cause such a one to waver. Steadfast is his mind, gained is deliverance. And the one who has considered all the contrasts on this earth and is no more disturbed by anything whatsoever in the world, the peaceful one, freed from anger, from sorrow and from longing, has passed beyond birth and death.

The extinction of greed, the extinction of anger, the extinction of delusion; this indeed is called Nirvana.

The Fourth Truth
The Noble Truth of the Path that Leads to the Extinction of Suffering

To give oneself up to indulgence in sensual pleasures, the base, the common, the vulgar, unholy, unprofitable, and also to give oneself up to self-mortification, the painful, unholy, unprofitable; both of these two extremes the Perfect One has avoided and found the Middle Path, which makes one both to see and to know and which leads to discernment, to peace, to enlightenment, to Nirvana.

It is the Noble Eightfold Path, the way that leads to the extinction of suffering, namely: Right Under-standing, Right Mindedness, Right Speech, Right Action, Right Living, Right Effort, Right Attentiveness *and Right Concentration.*

This is the Middle Path that the Perfect One has found, which leads to peace, to discernment, to enlightenment, to Nirvana.

Free from pain and torture is this path, free from suffering; it is the Perfect Path.

Give ear then, for the Immortal is found. I reveal, I set forth the Truth. As I reveal it to you, so Act!

The Eight Noble Steps to End Suffering

The Eight Noble Steps to End Suffering

First Step
Right Understanding

What now is Right Understanding? To understand suffering, to understand the origins of suffering, to understand the extinction of suffering and to understand the path that leads to the extinction of suffering; this is called Right Understanding. Or, when the noble disciple understands what demerit is and the root of demerit, what merit is and the root of merit, then also he has Right Understanding.

What now is demerit? Killing is demerit, stealing is demerit, lying is demerit, harsh language is demerit, frivolous talk and tale-bearing is demerit, sexual misconduct is demerit, using intoxicants is demerit, covetousness is demerit, ill-will is demerit, wrong views are demerit.

And what now is the root of demerit? Greed is a root of demerit. Anger is a root of demerit. Delusion, or false judgement, is a root of demerit. Therefore, I say to you that these de-meritorious things are of three kinds: either due to greed, or due to anger, or due to delusion.

What now is merit? To abstain from killing is merit, to abstain from stealing is merit, to abstain from lying is merit, to abstain from harsh language is merit, to abstain from frivolous talk and tale-bearing is merit, to abstain from using intoxicants is merit, absence of covetousness is merit, absence of ill-will is merit, right understanding is merit.

And what now is the root of merit? Absence of greed is a root of merit. Absence of anger is a root of merit. Absence of delusion is a root of merit. Or, when one understands that form, feeling, perception, mental formations and consciousness are transient, subject to suffering and without an Ego, also in that case one possesses Right Understanding.

Verily, because beings, obstructed by ignorance and ensnared by craving, now here, now there, seek ever-fresh delight, therefore one comes to ever-fresh rebirth.

And the action that is done out of greed, anger or delusion, that springs from them, has its source and origin there. This action ripens wherever one is reborn, and wherever this action ripens, there one will experience the fruits of this action, be it in this life, or be it in the next life, or be it in any other future life.

However, through the fading away of delusions, through the arising of wisdom, through the extinction of craving, no future rebirth takes place again. For the actions which are not done out of greed, anger or delusion, which have not sprung from them, which do not

The Eight Noble Steps to End Suffering

have their source and origin there, such actions as these are, through the absence of greed, anger and delusion, abandoned, rooted out like a palm tree torn out of the soil, destroyed and not liable to spring up again. In this respect one might rightly say of me that I teach annihilation, and that I herein train my disciples.

Certainly, I teach annihilation; the annihilation, namely, of Greed, Anger and Delusion, as well as the annihilation of the manifold evil and de-meritorious things.

Second Step
Right Mindedness

What now is Right Mindedness? The thought free from lust, the thought free from ill-will, the thought free from cruelty; this is called Right Mindedness.

Now, in understanding wrong-mindedness as wrong and right-mindedness as right, one practices Right Understanding, and in making efforts to overcome evil-mindedness and to arouse right-mindedness, one practices Right Effort. And in overcoming evil-mindedness with attentive mind, and dwelling with attentive mind in possession of right-mindedness, one practices Right Attentiveness.

The Dharma of the Buddha

Hence, there are three things that accompany and follow upon Right Mindedness, namely: Right Understanding, Right Effort and Right Attentiveness.

Third Step
Right Speech

What now is Right Speech? There, someone avoids lying and abstains from it. He speaks the truth, is devoted to the truth, reliable, worthy of confidence, is not a deceiver of people. Being at a meeting, or among people, or in the company of his relatives, or in society, or in the king's court, and called upon and asked as a witness to tell what he knows, he answers, if he knows nothing, 'I know nothing' and if he knows he answers, 'I know.' If he has seen nothing he answers, 'I have seen nothing' and if he has seen he answers, 'I have seen.' Thus, he never knowingly speaks a lie, neither for the sake of his own advantage, nor for the sake of another person's advantage, nor for the sake of any advantage whatsoever.

He avoids tale bearing and abstains from it. What he has heard here, he does not repeat there, so as to cause dissention there. What he has heard there, he does not repeat here, so as to cause dissention here.

The Eight Noble Steps to End Suffering

Thus, he unites those that are divided, and those that are united he encourages. Concord gladdens him. He delights and rejoices in concord, and it is concord that he spreads by his words.

He avoids harsh language and abstains from it. He speaks such words as are gentle, soothing to the ear, loving, going to the heart, courteous and dear, and agreeable to many.

He avoids vain talk and abstains from it. He speaks at the right time, in accordance with the facts, speaks what is useful, speaks about the Law and the Discipline. His speech is like a treasure, moderate and full of sense. This is called Right Speech.

Fourth Step
Right Action

What now is Right Action? There someone avoids the killing of living beings and abstains from it. Without stick or sword, conscientious, full of sympathy, he is anxious for the welfare of all living beings.

He avoids stealing and abstains from it. What another person possesses of goods and chattels in the village or in the wood; that he does not take away with thievish intent.

The Dharma of the Buddha

He avoids unlawful sexual intercourse and abstains from it. He has no intercourse with such women as are still under the protection of father, mother, brother, sister or relatives, nor with married women, nor with female monks, nor with engaged girls. This is called Right Action.

Fifth Step
Right Living

What now is Right Living? When the noble disciple, avoiding a wrong living, gets his livelihood by a right way of living; this is called Right Living.

One must not engage in any business that involves cruelty or injustice to either human beings or animals.

His life must be free from acquisitiveness, deceit and dishonesty.

He must have nothing to do with wars, gambling, prostitution or trading in poisons.

It must be a life of service rather than a life of profit and indulgence.

For those who wish to devote their entire attention to enlightenment, it must be a life free from all dependence or responsibility for property, family life or society.

The Eight Noble Steps to End Suffering

Sixth Step
Right Effort

What now is Right Effort? There are Four Great Efforts: the Effort to Avoid, the Effort to Overcome, the Effort to Develop and the Effort to Maintain.

What now is the Effort to Avoid? There the disciple incites his mind to avoid the arising of de-meritorious things that have not yet arisen, and he strives, puts forth his energy, strains his mind and struggles. And he strives to ward off greed, anger and delusion; that through which evil and de-meritorious things would arise if he remained with unguarded senses. And he watches over his senses, restrains his senses. Possessed of this noble control over the senses, he experiences inwardly a feeling of joy, into which no evil thing can enter. This is called the Effort to Avoid.

What now is the Effort to Overcome? There the disciple incites his mind to overcome the evil and de-meritorious things that have already arisen, and he strives, puts forth his energy, strains his mind and struggles. He does not retain any thought of sensual lust, ill-will or grief, or any other evil and de-meritorious states that may have arisen. He abandons them, dispels them, causes them to disappear. If, while regarding a certain object, there arise, on account of it, in the disciple evil and de-meritorious thoughts connected with greed, anger or delusion, then the disciple should gain another and wholesome object. Or, he should reflect on the misery of these thoughts, 'Unwholesome truly are these thoughts! Blammable are these thoughts! Of painful results are these thoughts!' Or, he should pay no attention to these thoughts. Or, he should consider the compounded nature of these thoughts. Or, with teeth clenched and tongue pressed against the gums, he should with all his mind restrain, suppress and root out these thoughts, and in doing so, these evil and de-meritorious thoughts connected with greed, anger or delusion will dissolve and disappear, and the mind will become settled and calm, composed and concentrated. This is called the Effort to Overcome.

What now is the Effort to Develop? There the disciple incites his will to arouse meritorious conditions that have not yet arisen, and he strives, puts forth his energy, strains his mind and struggles. Thus, he develops the Elements of Enlightenment, bent on solitude, on detachment, on extinction and ending in deliverance, namely: Attentiveness, Investigation of the Law, Energy, Rapture, Tranquility, Concentration and

The Eight Noble Steps to End Suffering

Equanimity. This is called the Effort to Develop.

What now is the Effort to Maintain? There the disciple incites his will to maintain the meritorious conditions that have already arisen, and not to let them disappear, but to bring them to growth, to maturity and to full perfection of development, and he strains, puts forth his energy, strains his mind and struggles. This is called the Effort to Maintain.

Seventh Step
Right Attentiveness

What now is Right Attentiveness? The way that leads to the attainment of purity, to the overcoming of sorrow and lamentation, to the end of pain and grief, to the entering upon the right path and the realization of Nirvana, are the Four Fundamentals of Attentiveness. And which are these Four? There the disciple lives in contemplation of the Body, in contemplation of the Feelings, in contemplation of the Mind and in contemplation of the Phenomena, ardent, clearly conscious and attentive, after putting away worldly greed and grief.

How does the disciple dwell in contemplation of the body? There the disciple retires to the forest, to the foot

31

*of a tree, or to a solitary place, sits himself down, with
legs crossed, body erect and with attentiveness fixed
before him. With attentive mind he breathes in, with
attentive mind he breathes out. When making a long
inhalation he knows, 'I make a long inhalation.' When
making a short inhalation he knows, 'I make a short
inhalation.' When making a long exhalation he knows,
'I make a long exhalation.' When making a short
exhalation he knows, 'I make a short exhalation.'
Clearly perceiving the entire breath body, he trains
himself. Thus, he dwells in contemplation of the body,
either in regard to his own person, or to other persons,
or to both. He beholds how the body arises, beholds
how it passes away. He beholds the arising and passing
away of the body.*

*Now, how does the disciple dwell in contemplation
of the feelings? In experiencing feelings the disciple
knows, 'I have an agreeable feeling' or 'I have a dis-
agreeable feeling' or 'I have an indifferent feeling.'
Thus, he dwells in contemplation of the feelings, either
with regard to his own person, or to other persons, or to
both. He beholds how the feelings arise, beholds how
they pass away. He beholds the arising and passing
away of the feelings. Feelings are there. This clear
consciousness is present in him and because of his*

knowledge and mindfulness he lives independently, unattached to anything in the world. Thus, does the disciple dwell in contemplation of the feelings.

And how does the disciple dwell in contemplation of the mind? There the disciple knows the greedy mind as greedy, and the generous mind as generous. He knows the angry mind as angry, and the compassionate mind as compassionate. He knows the deluded mind as deluded, and the conscious mind as conscious. He knows the composed mind as composed, and the scattered mind as scattered, knows the developed mind as developed, and the undeveloped mind as undeveloped, knows the concentrated mind as concentrated and the unconcentrated mind as unconcentrated, knows the freed mind as freed and the enslaved mind as enslaved. Thus, does the disciple dwell in contemplation of the mind.

Now, how does the disciple dwell in contemplation of the phenomena? There the disciple dwells in contemplation of the Five Hindrances. He knows when there is Lust in him, 'In me is lust.' He knows when there is Anger in him, 'In me is anger.' He knows when there is Torpor and Drowsiness in him, 'In me is torpor and drowsiness.' He knows when there is Restlessness and Mental Worry in him, 'In me is restlessness and

mental worry.' He knows when there are Doubts in
him, 'In me are doubts.' He knows when these hindrances are not in him, 'In me these hindrances are
not.' He knows how they come to arise and knows
how, once arisen, they are overcome. He knows how,
once overcome, they do not arise again in the future.

And further, the disciple dwells in contemplation of
the phenomena, namely of the Five Aggregates of Existence. He knows what Bodily Form is and how it arises
and passes away, knows what Feeling is and how it
arises and passes away, knows what Perception is
and how it arises and passes away, knows what the
Mental Formations are and how they arise and pass
away, and he knows what Consciousness is and how it
arises and passes away.

And further, the disciple dwells in contemplation
of the phenomena, namely, of the Seven Elements of
Enlightenment. The disciple knows when there is
Attentiveness in him, knows when there is Investigation of the Law in him, knows when there is Enthu-
siasm in him, knows when there is Tranquility in him,
knows when there is Concentration in him, and he
knows when there is Equanimity in him. He knows
when these are not in him. He knows how they arise
and are fully developed. Thus, does the disciple dwell

*in contemplation of the phenomena, either with regard
to his own person, or to other persons, or to both. He
beholds how the phenomena arise, beholds how they
pass away. He beholds the arising and passing away
of the phenomena.*

*Phenomena are there. This clear consciousness is
present in him and because of his knowledge and
mindfulness he lives independent, unattached to
anything in the world.*

Eighth Step
Right Concentration

*What now is Right Concentration? Fixation of the
mind to a single object is called concentration. The
Four Fundamentals of Attentiveness should be the objects of concentration. The practicing, developing and
cultivating of these things is called the Development of
Concentration.*

*Detached from sensual objects, detached from de-
meritorious conditions, the disciple enters the first
trance, which is accompanied by verbal thought and
rumination, is born of detachment and is filled with
rapture and happiness. This first trance is free from
five things and five things are present. When the*

disciple enters the first trance, there have vanished in him the Five Hindrances: Lust, Anger and Ill-will, Torpor and Drowsiness, Restlessness and Mental Worry, Doubts; and there are present in him: Verbal Thought, Rumination, Rapture, Happiness and Concentration.

And further, after the subsiding of verbal thought and rumination, and by the gaining of inward tranquilization and oneness of mind, the disciple enters into a state free from verbal thought and rumination. He enters into the second trance, which is born of concentration and filled with rapture and happiness.

And further, after the fading away of rapture, he dwells in equanimity, attentive, clearly conscious, and he experiences in his person that feeling of which the noble ones say, 'happy lives the one of equanimity and attentive mind.' Thus, he enters the third trance.

And further, after the giving up of pleasure and pain, and through the disappearance of previous joy and grief, he enters into a state beyond pleasure and pain. He enters into the fourth trance, which is purified by equanimity and attentiveness.

Develop your concentration, for the one who has concentration understands things according to their reality. And what are those things? They are the arising *and passing away of bodily form, feeling, perception, mental formations and states of consciousness.*

Thus, these Five Aggregates of Existence must be wisely penetrated. Delusion and Craving must be wisely abandoned, and Tranquility and Insight must be wisely developed.

This is the Middle Path, which the Perfect One has discovered, and which makes one both to see and to know, which leads to Peace, to Discernment, to Enlightenment, ...to Nirvana.

The Dhammapada

The Dhammapada

The Twin Verses

All that we are is a result of what we have thought; it is founded on our thoughts and it is made up of our thoughts. If a person speaks or acts with an evil thought, suffering will follow him as the wheel follows the hoof of the beast that draws the carriage.

All that we are is a result of what we have thought; it is founded on our thoughts and it is made up of our thoughts. If a person speaks or acts with a good thought, happiness will follow him like a shadow that never leaves him.

'He abused me, he beat me, he robbed me.' Harbor these thoughts and your hatred and your suffering will never cease.

'He abused me, he beat me, he robbed me.' Abandon these thoughts and your hatred and your suffering will cease.

Hatred does not cease by hatred. Hatred only ceases by love. This is an Eternal Law.

Some do not admit that everyone must die one day. Quarrels cease for those who acknowledge this truth.

The Dhammapada

The one who lives only for pleasure with his senses uncontrolled, and who is immoderate, idle and weak, will surely be overthrown by Mara, the tempter, as the wind overthrows a feeble tree.

Mara, the tempter, cannot overthrow the one who lives without seeking pleasure, whose senses are well guarded, and who is moderate, faithful and strong, just as the wind cannot overthrow a rocky mountain.

The one who has not cleansed himself from sin, and who disregards temperance and truth, is not worthy to wear the orange-colored robe of the monk.

But the one who has cleansed himself from sin, and also regards temperance and truth, is indeed worthy to wear the orange-colored robe of the monk.

Those who see truth where there is no truth, and see untruth in the truth, never arrive at reality, but follow vain desires.

Those who know the truth as the truth, and the untruth as the untruth, see reality and follow their true nature.

As rain breaks through an ill-thatched house, so desires will break through an ill-trained mind.

As rain does not enter into a well-thatched house, so desires will not enter into a well-trained mind.

The Dhammapada

*The fool suffers both in this world and the next.
He suffers when he experiences the fruits of his bad
deeds.*

*The wise person delights in both this world
and the next. He is filled with happiness when he
experiences the fruits of his good deeds.*

*The fool suffers in both this world and the next.
He suffers when he thinks about the evil he has done,
and he is even more miserable when following the evil
path.*

*The wise person is happy in both this world and
the next. He is happy when he thinks about the good
he has done, and he is happier still when following the
good path.*

*The thoughtless person who talks about the
Law but does not follow the Path is like a cowman
counting the cows of others, but who does not have any
of his own.*

*The thoughtful person who can recite little of
the Law, but who possesses true knowledge and serenity
of mind, unattached to anything in this world, is
indeed a follower of the Path.*

The Dhammapada

Meditation

Meditation is the path of immortality, thoughtlessness is the path of death. Those who meditate do not die, but those who are thoughtless and do not meditate are already like the dead.

Those who are watchful delight in meditation and rejoice in the knowledge of the Elect.

These wise people who are meditative, steady and of high moral character, will reach Nirvana, the highest happiness.

If a meditative person is alert and not forgetful, and if his deeds are pure and he is considerate, restraining his senses and living in accordance with the Law, then his happiness will increase beyond measure.

By awakening oneself, by meditation, by restraint and control over the senses, the wise person will make of himself an island, which no flood can overtake.

Fools seek after riches. The wise consider meditation to be their most valuable jewel.

Do not follow the evil path! The one who reflects and meditates will receive ample joy, even in this life.

The Dhammapada

When the wise person drives away vanity by way of meditation he looks down upon the fools, as a man who stands on a mountain looks down upon those who live close to the ground.

Meditating among the thoughtless, awake among the sleepers, the wise advance like a racer behind an old worn out horse.

People praise earnestness. Thoughtlessness is always condemned.

A seeker, who delights in meditation and who looks upon thoughtlessness with aversion, rages like a fire and burns through all his fetters.

Thoughts

As a fletcher straightens his arrows, likewise a wise person straightens his trembling and unsteady mind, which is so very hard to control.

Thoughts tremble and thrash about like a fish out of water when trying to escape the grip of Mara, the tempter.

It is good to tame a mind that, now here, now there, wanders everywhere. A tame mind brings great happiness.

Let the wise be watchful and guard their thoughts. Thoughts well guarded bring happiness.

Those who put a bridle on their wandering thoughts will free themselves from their fetters.

If a person's thoughts are unsteady and unaware, then he will never find the Path.

An unfettered mind, a mind that no longer places judgements, has no fear.

Knowing that the body is as fragile as a jar, the wise person makes the mind as firm as a fortress, and wisdom will protect him from the snares of Mara, the tempter.

Before long this body will lie on the ground like a useless log, without understanding or consciousness.

Whatever a hater may do to another hater, or an enemy to an enemy, a wrongly directed mind will do greater harm.

Not a mother, nor a father, nor any other relatives will do more good for you than your own well directed mind.

Flowers

Who will overcome this world and the world of the dead? Who will find the shining Path, as a gardener finds the rarest flower?

The Dhammapada

You will overcome this world and the world of the dead. As a gardener finds the rarest flower, so you will discover the shining Path and transcend this world.

Those who look upon this world as a mirage will break through the flowery arrows of craving and will never meet the King of Death.

Death carries away a thoughtless and distracted person, as a flood carries away a sleeping village.

While the thoughtless person gathers the flowers of pleasure, he will be overtaken by death before he can ever be satisfied.

As the bee collects nectar and departs without injuring the color or scent of the flower, so should the sage live harmlessly in this world.

The sage should not take notice of the failures of others, or of their sins of commission or omission, but rather, he should look instead at his own shortcomings.

Like a beautiful flower full of color but without scent, are the fruitless words of those who speak about the Path, but do not act accordingly.

Like a beautiful flower full of color and scent, are the fruitful words of those who speak about the Path, and act accordingly.

The Dhammapada

As many kinds of wreaths that can be made from a pile of flowers, so should the disciple do as many good deeds.

The scent of flowers, sandalwood and jasmine does not travel against the wind, but the scent of good deeds travels everywhere.

The scent of good works is sweeter than any incense, jasmine or flowers.

The scent of jasmine, incense and flowers travels a small distance, but the scent of goodness rises to heaven.

Mara, the tempter, cannot conquer those who live thoughtfully and who are made free through true knowledge.

As a lily grows among a heap of rubbish along the highway and lightens the hearts of people with its sweet perfume, so likewise the enlightened ones will lighten the hearts among people who walk in darkness.

The Fool

The night is long for the sentry. The road is long for the weary traveler. This life is long for the fool who spends many lives looking for the Truth.

The Dhammapada

If a wise traveler cannot find another wise
person to accompany him then he should go alone.
It is better to travel alone than to travel with a fool.

The fool thinks, 'These children and this wealth
belong to me.' But how can he control children and
wealth when he cannot control his own mind?

The fool who knows his foolishness is wise so
far, but the fool who thinks himself wise is foolish
indeed.

Though a fool may know a wise person all his
life, he will perceive the Truth as little as the spoon
savors the taste of the soup.

But a thoughtful person who knows a wise
person even for just one minute will perceive the Truth,
even as the tongue savors the taste of the soup.

Fools are their own worst enemies. Their evil
deeds bear the fruit of their own destruction.

Bad deeds bring great remorse. The fruit of
those deeds is reaped in sorrow.

Good deeds bring great reward. The fruit of
those deeds is reaped in joy.

As long as the evil deed has not ripened, the fool
thinks his deed is as sweet as honey. But when the fruit
of that deed ripens, then that fool suffers miserably.

The Dhammapada

Although a fool fasts and eats his food with the tip of a blade of grass, he is still not worth the smallest part of those to whom the food is the Path.

A bad deed does not suddenly curdle like milk. Instead it follows the fool slowly, like a smoldering fire.

The bad deed, after ripening, brings suffering to the fool. Then it destroys his own happiness and cuts him off at his roots.

The fool wishes for worldly fame, success and recognition. He wants others to worship and respect him. 'May both laymen and monks praise and obey me.' These are the thoughts of the fool, and so his desires and his pride increase.

This road leads to wealth and worldly success, the other road is the path to Nirvana. If the seeker who follows the way of the enlightened has learned this, then he will not yearn for praise from others, but instead he will strive after separation from this world.

The Wise

If you meet a wise person who shows you where you are mistaken, then look upon that person as a treasure. It is good to know such a person.

The Dhammapada

Let the wise person advise others and keep those people from committing errors. He will be loved by the good, and only the bad will hate him.

Do not keep foolish company! Instead keep wise company, because people are known by the company they keep.

The one who lives according to the Law lives happily with a serene mind. The sage always rejoices in the Law, as preached by the Elect.

Irrigators guide water, fletchers straighten arrows, carpenters turn wood, and wise people shape themselves.

Just as a solid rock is not moved by the wind, so wise people are not moved by praise or blame.

Wise people, after listening to the Law, become serene, like a deep, smooth and still lake.

The wise walk on, neither touched by happiness nor sorrow. The wise never appear elated or depressed.

Neither for his own sake, nor for the sake of others, will a wise person wish for a family or wealth. The wise never wish to gain by another's loss.

Few people arrive at the other shore. Most run up and down this side of the torrent.

The Dhammapada

Those who, after hearing the Truth, follow the Law, will pass across the realm of death, which is so difficult to overcome.

A wise person should not walk in the darkness of an ordinary life, but should walk in the brightness of the life of a follower of the Path. He leaves all worldly pleasures behind and, calling nothing his own, the wise person frees himself from all the troubles of the mind.

Those whose minds are well grounded in the knowledge of the Law and who have given up all attachments in this world, who rejoice without clinging to anything and have overcome their cravings are free, even in this world.

The Venerable

There is no suffering for the one who has completed the journey, who has abandoned grief and has cut off all desires.

Like a swan that rises from the lake, the sage moves onward with his thoughts at peace.

Those who have not collected wealth and stores of food live like the birds in the air. They have perceived the Void, the Unconditioned, the Absolute.

The Dhammapada

The path of the one whose passions have been stilled, who does not seek enjoyment and who has perceived the Void is difficult to understand, like the path of the birds in the air.

Even the heavenly beings envy the one whose senses have been controlled, like well-broken horses. The one who is free from pride has cut his fetters.

Such a one as this is tolerant like the earth. He is like a lake without mud, and no new birth waits for him.

His thoughts are quiet, and his words and deeds are likewise quiet. He becomes a quiet person once he has obtained freedom by true knowledge.

The one who has cut off all attachments, removed all temptations and renounced all desires is truly great among people.

Whether in a village or in a forest, on water or dry land, wherever venerable people dwell, that place is delightful.

Delightful are those forests where the world finds no delight! There the passionless ones live happily, wanting nothing.

The Dhammapada

The Thousands

One word of sense, which brings the listener peace, is worth more than a thousand senseless words.

One verse of a poem, which brings the listener peace, is worth more than a thousand senseless verses.

It is better to conquer oneself than to conquer a thousand times a thousand men in battle. The person who conquers himself is the greatest of warriors.

Not even the heavenly beings can challenge the victory of a person who has conquered himself and who always lives under restraint of the senses.

It is better to pay homage to an awakened person for one moment than to offer sacrifices for a thousand years.

Whatever someone sacrifices in this world in order to gain merit, it is not worth even one moment of reverence shown to the righteous.

Those who revere a righteous person will receive, even in this life, abundant beauty, happiness and strength.

It is better to live one day of a virtuous and reflecting life than to exist for a thousand years with unrestrained senses.

The Dhammapada

It is better to live one day with strength and determination than to exist for a thousand years in idleness and weakness.

It is better to live one day in understanding of the Truth than to exist for a thousand years without such understanding.

Evil

It is better to do good than to do evil. If someone hesitates to do what is good, then his mind is easily seized by mischief.

If someone commits a sin, let him avoid doing it again. He should not delight in mischief. Pain and suffering is the outcome of evil.

If someone does a good deed, let him do it again and again. Happiness is the outcome of good.

Even a fool is happy as long as his evil deed has not ripened. But when his evil deed has ripened, then he suffers.

Even a good person experiences bad days, as long as his good deed has not ripened. But when his good deed has ripened, then he is happy.

The Dhammapada

Let no one think lightly of evil and say to himself, 'It cannot touch me.' Even as, drop by drop, water fills the pitcher, so little by little the fool is filled with demerit.

Let no one think lightly of good and say to himself, 'It cannot be for me.' Even as, drop by drop, water fills the pitcher, so little by little the wise person is filled with merit.

Let someone avoid evil, as a wealthy merchant avoids a dangerous road and as a man who loves life avoids poison.

A man who has no wounds on his hand may touch poison without being harmed. The poison will not harm those who have no wounds, just as evil will not overtake the one who commits no evil.

Suffering will fall back upon the fool who harms the harmless, like dust thrown against the wind.

Some people are reborn, evildoers go into hell, righteous people go into heaven, and those who are free from all worldly desires enter Nirvana.

Not in the sky, nor in the middle of the sea, nor in a cave in the mountains, is there a place where death cannot overtake the fool.

The Dhammapada

Punishment

All people fear pain and death. Remembering this, let no one strike or kill another.

The one who punishes or kills another who longs for happiness will not find happiness for himself.

Do not speak harshly to another. Those who are spoken to in this way will answer in the same manner. Angry words bring great remorse.

You should remain quiet, like a broken trumpet. You will reach Nirvana when anger is no longer in you.

As a cowman gathers the cattle into the stable, so old age and death gather all before them.

A fool is unaware that his evil deeds are igniting the fire that will consume him.

A person who inflicts pain on innocent and harmless beings will come to one of these ten states:

He will have cruel suffering, injury to the body, a severe illness, insanity,

Trouble with the authorities, a dreadful accusation, death of relatives, loss of wealth,

Or a fire will burn down his house, and when he dies he will go into the hell-state.

The Dhammapada

Not nakedness, nor matted hair, nor fasting or laying on the ground, nor by rubbing himself with dust can purify someone who has not overcome his desires.

Even someone who is rich can attain enlightenment if he exercises tranquility, is subdued, restrained, chaste, and has stopped judging others.

Is there, in this world, any person so restrained that he gives no occasion for reproach, as a well-trained horse never deserves the whip?

Like a well-trained horse when touched by the whip, you should be active and lively, and by faith, virtue, energy, meditation and discernment of the Law you will overcome reproach. By perfection of knowledge and restraint of the senses, you will never be forgetful.

Old Age

How is there laughter, how is there joy, when this world is always burning? Why do you, who are surrounded by darkness, not seek a light?

Look at this dressed up lump, covered with wounds, joined together, sickly, full of vain thoughts, which has no strength, no hold!

The Dhammapada

*This body is wasted, full of sickness and frail.
This heap of corruption breaks to pieces. The life in it
must die.*

*These white bones, like empty husks, are
scattered in the autumn. What pleasure is there, then,
in looking at them?*

*After the framework for the body has been
made by the bones it is covered with flesh and blood.
And in it dwells old age and death, pride and
hypocrisy.*

*As the brilliant chariots of kings are destroyed
in battle, so likewise this body is destroyed by old age,
but the virtues of good people are never destroyed.*

*A person who has learned little grows old like
an ox. His flesh grows, but his knowledge does not
grow.*

*I have run through a course of many births
looking for the maker of this tabernacle. And birth is so
painful, again and again. But now, the maker of this
tabernacle has been seen and this body will not be born
again. All the rafters have been broken, the ridgepole is
shattered and my mind has forsaken all desires.*

*People who have wasted their lives away and
learned nothing perish like old herons in a lake without
fish.*

The Dhammapada

People who have wasted their lives away and learned nothing lie like broken bows, sighing after the past.

The Self

If someone holds himself dear, let him be watchful. A wise person will be watchful at least part of the night.

If a wise person wants to teach others, then first he should direct himself to what is right. In this way, no one will suffer.

Self is the master of Self. Who else can be the master of the Self? With the Self well controlled, another master is hard to find.

The mischief done by the fool, self-begotten and self-bred, crushes the fool, as a diamond crushes a precious stone.

Like a creeper that surrounds a tree, the evil deeds of the fool will bring him down to a state where even his enemies wish him to be.

Bad deeds, and deeds that are harmful to ourselves are easy to do. To do what is beneficial and good is very difficult.

The Dhammapada

The fool who scorns the teachings of the Elect and follows the false teachings is like the bamboo tree. He bears the fruit of his own destruction.

By oneself evil is done, by oneself one suffers. By oneself evil is left undone, by oneself one is purified.

Let no one forget his own duty for the sake of another's, however great. Let someone discover his life's work and attend to it with all his heart.

The World

Do not follow the evil path! Do not live in thoughtlessness! Do not follow false teachings! Do not be a friend of this world.

Rouse yourself! Do not be idle! Follow the law of virtue! The virtuous live happily in this world and the next.

Look upon this world as a mirage. The King of Death cannot touch those who view the world in this way.

Come, look at this glittering world! It is like a royal chariot. Fools are immersed in it, but the wise do not touch it.

The Dhammapada

One who was formerly reckless and afterward becomes sober brightens up this world, like the moon when freed from the clouds.

One whose evil deeds have been covered over with good deeds brightens up this world, like the moon when freed from the clouds.

This world is dark, and only a few can see it. These few go into heaven, like birds that have escaped from the net.

The swans go on the path of the sun. They go through the ether by means of their miraculous power. The wise are led out of this world, when they have conquered Mara and his evil train.

If someone transgresses the Law and speaks lies and scoffs at the belief in another world, then there is no evil he will not do.

The uncharitable do not go into heaven. Only a fool does not praise generosity. A wise person rejoices in charity, and through it becomes blessed in the other world.

Better than sovereignty over the entire world, better than going into heaven, better than lordship over all worlds, is the first step on the Holy Path.

The Dhammapada

The Awakened

One whose conquest is over, who has forsaken all desires, by what path can this awakened one be lead astray?

Even the heavenly beings envy those who are awake and not forgetful, who are given to meditation, who are wise and delight in retirement from this world.

Not to commit any sin, to do good and to purify one's mind; this is the teaching of the awakened.

The awakened ones call patience the highest virtue. One is not an anchorite who strikes others, and one is not an ascetic who insults others.

Not to blame, not to strike, to live restrained under the Law, to be moderate in the senses and to dwell on the highest thoughts; this is the teaching of the awakened.

There is no satisfying lust, even with a shower of gold pieces. The one who knows that lusts have a short taste and cause pain is wise.

The disciple who is fully awakened finds no satisfaction even in heavenly pleasures, but delights only in the destruction of all desires.

The Dhammapada

*People, driven by fear, go to many a refuge.
They go to mountains and forests, to sacred groves and
sacred trees.*

*But this is not a safe refuge. This is not the best
refuge. A person is not delivered from suffering after
having gone to such a refuge as this.*

*One who takes refuge with the Buddha, with
the Dharma and with the Sangha, and who with clear
understanding sees the Four Noble Truths:*

*The truth of suffering, the truth of the origin of
suffering, the truth of the extinction of suffering and
the truth of the eight noble steps that lead to the
extinction of suffering:*

*That person has taken the best refuge. Having
gone to that refuge, the disciple is delivered from all
pain and suffering.*

*A Buddha, or supernatural person, is not easily
found. He is not born everywhere. Wherever such a
sage is born, that race prospers.*

*Happy is the birth of the Awakened One!
Happy is the teaching of the True Law! Happy is the
sangha that follows the Awakened One and happy are
the followers that are at peace!*

The Dhammapada

Merit is measureless for those who pay homage to those who deserve homage, whether the awakened or their disciples, and for those who have overcome the host of Mara and have crossed the flood of sorrow, who have found deliverance and know no fear.

Happiness

Let us live happily, not hating those who hate!
Let us live happily, not judging those who judge!
Let us live happily, healthy among the sick!
Let us live happily, generous among the greedy!
Let us live happily, though we call nothing our own! Let us live like the heavenly beings, feeding on love.

Victory breeds hatred because the conquered are unhappy. The one who has given up both victory and defeat is happy.

There is no fire like passion, there is no ill will like hatred, there is no pain like this body, and there is no happiness like Nirvana.

Craving is the worst disease and this body brings the greatest of pains. Giving up both craving and the pain of this body brings Nirvana, the highest happiness.

The Dhammapada

The one who has tasted the sweetness of solitude and tranquility is free from fear and free from impurity. He tastes the sweetness of drinking from the Law.

The sight of the Elect is happiness and to live with them is pure bliss. If a person does not associate with fools, but instead follows the wise, then he will be happy.

The one who walks in the company of fools will suffer for a long time. Company with fools, as with an enemy, is always painful. Company with the wise is pleasurable, like meeting with friends.

Therefore, one ought to follow the wise, the intelligent, the learned, the enduring, the dutiful, the Elect. One ought to follow a good and wise person, as the moon follows the path of the stars.

Pleasure

The one who gives himself over to pleasure and does not give himself to meditation will end up envying the one who meditates.

Let no one look for what is pleasant or unpleasant. Not to see what is pleasant is painful, and to see the unpleasant is also painful.

The Dhammapada

Therefore, let no one cling to anything. Those who have gone beyond the loved and the hated have cut all their fetters.

From pleasure springs grief, and from pleasure springs fear. The one who is free from pleasure knows neither grief nor fear.

From clinging springs grief, and from clinging springs fear. The one who is free from clinging knows neither grief nor fear.

From lust springs grief, and from lust springs fear. The one who is free from lust knows neither grief nor fear.

From greed springs grief, and from greed springs fear. The one who is free from greed knows neither grief nor fear.

People hold dear the one who possesses virtue and intelligence, who is just, speaks the truth and minds his own business.

The one who is enlightened and free from craving, whose only desire is the attainment of Nirvana, will be called, 'One who is carried up by the stream.'

Family, friends and the beloved greet the person who has been away on a long journey and returns home safe.

In the same manner, good works will receive the one who has done good and has left this world for the other world, just as kinsmen receive a friend on his return.

Anger

Let those who overcome their bondage forsake anger and pride. Suffering cannot touch those who are not attached to anything and call nothing their own.

The one who holds back rising anger like a rolling chariot is a true driver. Others merely hold the reins.

Let people overcome anger by love. Let them overcome evil by good, greed by generosity, and lying by telling the truth!

Speak the truth and do not give in to anger. Give from whatever little you possess to those who ask and your reward will be great in heaven.

The sage who does not injure anyone and who always controls his senses will go to the state of Nirvana, a place where all sufferings cease.

Passions will come to an end for those who are always watchful, who meditate day and night, and who strive after Nirvana.

The Dhammapada

This is an old saying: 'People blame those who are quiet, they blame those who speak much, and they blame those who say little.' There is no one who is never blamed.

People give blame or praise. No one is always blamed or always praised.

But those, who people praise continually day after day, who are without blemish, wise, rich in knowledge and virtue, who would dare blame them, who are like a coin made of the purest gold? Even the heavenly beings praise them.

Beware of anger in your body and control your body! Leave the sins of the body and practice virtue instead.

Beware of anger in your speech and control your speech! Leave the sins of the tongue and practice virtue instead.

Beware of anger in your mind and control your mind! Leave the sins of the mind and practice virtue instead.

The wise ones who control their body, speech and minds are indeed masters of themselves.

The Dhammapada

Impurity

When the messenger of Death comes for you don't be caught standing at the door of your departure unprepared, with no provisions for the journey.

Make of yourself an island, meditate and be wise! When your impurities have been removed and you are free from guilt, then you will enter into the heavenly world of the Elect and never again enter into birth and decay.

Let a wise person remove the impurities of his soul, as a silversmith occasionally removes the impurities in the silver.

The rust that arises out of the iron destroys it. In the same way evil destroys the fool who commits evil.

Prayers are rusted when they are not spoken, houses are spoiled when repairs are neglected, the body is tainted by sloth, and the watchman is ruined by his thoughtlessness.

When a woman lacks loyalty and a man lacks generosity, then there is impurity in this world and the next.

The Dhammapada

Ignorance is the greatest spoiler of all. Remove the taint of ignorance and be free!

One who destroys life, who speaks lies, who takes what is not given to him, who seduces another man's wife,

And the one who gives himself to drinking intoxicating liquors will, even in this life, dig up his own roots.

Know that the unrestrained are in a bad state. Take heed so that greediness and unrestraint of the senses do not bring suffering upon you for a long time!

The one who envies the talents of others will never find peace of mind for himself.

The one in whom the root of envy is destroyed will find peace of mind by day and by night.

There is no snare like craving, no fire like hatred, and no rushing river like greed.

To find fault with others is easy, but to find fault with oneself is difficult to perceive. A person hides their own faults, as a cheat hides the bad dice from the gambler.

If someone looks for the faults in others his own faults will increase, and he will be very far from being free of them.

The Dhammapada

There is no path to freedom for those whose thoughts are only for this world. This world delights in vanity, but the awakened take no part in it.

The Just

A person is not just if he judges too harshly. The one who judges fairly and leads others, not by violence, but by the Law, is called Just.

A person is not wise because he has much to say. The one who is patient, free from hatred and fear, is called wise.

A man is not an 'Elder' just because his hair is gray. His age may be ripe, but he is called 'old in vain.'

An 'Elder' is one in whom there is truth, virtue, restraint, moderation, freedom from impurity and wisdom.

An envious, greedy, dishonest person does not become respectable by means of speaking many words or by their physical beauty.

One in whom envy, greed and dishonesty has been destroyed, pulled out by the very roots and has been replaced by wisdom, is called 'respectable.'

The Dhammapada

An undisciplined person who speaks lies cannot be made into a monk by simply wearing the orange-colored robe. How can someone who is still held captive by desires and greed be a monk?

One who has quieted his mind and given up all desires can be called a monk.

A person is not a bhikshu simply because he depends upon the charity of others. Someone is a bhikshu because he adopts the Law of the Buddha, not because he begs.

The one who has gone beyond good and evil, who is chaste and who passes through this world with knowledge is indeed a bhikshu.

A person is not a sage simply because he is silent. The true sage takes the Middle Path, chooses good and avoids evil, weighs both sides and judges fairly.

A person who injures living creatures, whether human or animal, is not called an 'Elect.' The Elect have pity on all living creatures, whether human or animal, and are anxious for their welfare.

The Dhammapada

Not only by discipline and vows, not only by much studying, not only by entering into a trance and sleeping alone can someone earn the happiness of Nirvana. A person receives enlightenment when he has reached the complete destruction of all desires.

The Way (The Path)

The best of paths is the Noble Eightfold Path. The best of truths are the Four Noble Truths. The best virtue is passionlessness, and the best person is the one who has the eyes to see this.

Follow the Noble Eightfold Path! This is the way that leads to purification of the mind.

There is no pain in following the Great Direct Way! It is the perfect path.

You yourself must make the effort. The Tathagatas only point the way. The thoughtful ones who enter on the Path are freed from the bondage of Mara, the tempter.

'All things are changing.' The one who understands this truth is freed from sorrow. This is the way to purity.

The Dhammapada

'All forms are formless and not real.' The one who understands this truth is free from grief and pain. This is the Shining Path.

Someone who is lazy, who, though young and strong is full of sloth, and whose will and thoughts are weak and idle, will never find the Path.

If someone controls his speech, restrains his mind and commits no sin with his body, then he will find the Way.

Through meditation wisdom grows and through lack of meditation wisdom is lost. Therefore, let the wise person choose the path of meditation and let his wisdom increase.

Cut down the whole forest of lust, not just the tree. From lust springs fear. When you have cut down every tree and shrub, then you will be free!

So long as a man lusts after a woman his mind is in bondage, like a calf tied to its mother for her milk.

Cut out the love of Self, as the autumn leaves of the lotus flower are cut. Cherish the road that leads to peace and you will find Nirvana.

'I will live here for the winter and there for the summer.' Thus thinks the fool, not considering his own death.

The Dhammapada

But death will come and carry away that fool,
as a flood carries away a sleeping village.

Neither friends nor relatives can save you from
death when his messenger has come to take you away.
Therefore, knowing this truth, a wise person should
quickly clear the way that leads to Nirvana.

Miscellaneous

If, by leaving a small pleasure one can see the
greater pleasure, then let the wise person leave the
sensual pleasures for the greater pleasure of Nirvana.

One who causes pain to others, entangled in the
bonds of hatred, will never find happiness for himself
and will never be freed from hatred.

When good works are neglected and bad deeds
are committed instead, then the suffering of unruly,
thoughtless people increases.

But suffering will end for the thoughtful ones,
whose watchfulness is always directed at restraint of
the senses, accomplishing good works and avoiding
mischief making.

An enlightened person, though in his mind has
killed both father and mother, along with valiant kings
and citizens is now, in his purity, free from guilt.

The Dhammapada

The disciples of the Buddha are always aware, and their minds delight in compassion by day and by night.

The disciples of the Buddha are always aware, and their minds delight in meditation by day and by night.

The disciples of the Buddha are always aware, and their thoughts are set on enlightenment by day and by night.

It is hard to leave the world and live the life of an ascetic. But it is just as hard to live in this world. Therefore, follow the path of the enlightened and be free from suffering.

A faithful, virtuous and prosperous person will be honored wherever he goes.

Good people shine from afar, like the snow capped mountains. Bad people are obscure, like arrows that are shot in the dark.

The one who meditates in retirement from the world will rejoice in the destruction of all desires.

The Downward Path

People who tell lies and avoid telling the truth go into the hell-state.

The Dhammapada

Many monks who wear the orange-colored robe are unrestrained and ill conditioned. Such monks as these will enter the hell-state.

It is better to swallow a red-hot ball of iron than to use others at their expense.

There are four things that will happen to the reckless man who seduces another man's wife:
he will get a bad reputation,
he will have trouble sleeping,
he will be punished by the authorities,
he will go into the hell-state.

The short pleasure of the frightened man in the arms of the frightened woman is not worth the punishment of the hell-state. Therefore, let no man seduce another man's wife.

As a blade of grass if clumsily grasped will cut the hand, so also the ascetic who lives a bad life will be cut down to the hell-state.

There is no reward for acting thoughtlessly, breaking vows and hesitating to do what is good.

Let someone vigorously attend to his duty. A careless and lazy seeker only scatters the dust of his passions.

The Dhammapada

It is better to leave an evil deed undone than to feel remorse afterwards. It is better to do a good deed and not feel remorseful.

Let someone guard himself like a well-guarded fort. Do not relax your watchfulness for even one moment, and in this way you will avoid being seized by mischief.

Those who are ashamed when there is no reason to be ashamed, and those who are not ashamed when there is reason to be ashamed are both wrong. Both are following a downward path.

Those who fear when there is nothing to fear, and those who do not fear when they should fear are both wrong. Both are following a downward path.

Those who see evil where there is no evil, and those who do not see evil where evil exists are both wrong. Both are following a downward path.

Those who see evil as evil and good as good see clearly and, embracing reality, they enter on the upward path.

The Dhammapada

The Elephant

Silently I shall endure abuse, as the elephant in battle endures the piercing arrow, for many people in this world are unkind.

A tamed elephant is led into battle. The king mounts a tamed elephant. Camels, horses and elephants are good, if tamed, but the person who tames himself is even better.

No one can enter Nirvana on the backs of tamed animals, but only by taming himself.

The elephant called Dhamapalaka, his temples running with sweat and difficult to hold, will not eat one morsel of food when bound. The elephant longs for the elephant grove.

The fool who becomes fat and lazy, lolling about like a hog, will be reborn again and again.

This mind of mine, which was formerly scattered and wandered aimlessly, is now held under my control, as a rider who holds the hook reins in the furious elephant.

Do not be thoughtless, guard your thoughts! Draw yourself out of the evil path, like an elephant draws himself out of the mud.

The Dhammapada

*Let someone find a wise companion to
accompany him and together they will live happily,
overcoming all dangers.*

*If someone cannot find a wise companion to
accompany him then let him travel alone, like a king
who has left his conquered country behind.*

*It is better to live alone than to live with a fool.
Let the wise person walk alone, avoiding wrongdoing,
with few desires, like the lonely elephant.*

*Friends are pleasant. Enjoyment of the time
spent with friends is pleasant. Doing good works is
pleasant at the hour of death, but most pleasant of all
is the end of all suffering.*

*Being a mother is a happy state, as is being a
father. But happiest of all is the state of enlightenment.*

*Goodness lasting into old age is pleasant.
Pleasant is a faith firmly rooted. Acquiring wisdom
is pleasant, but the most pleasant of all is avoiding
wrong doing.*

Thirst (Craving)

*The thirst of a thoughtless person grows like a
creeper. He runs here and there, like a monkey seeking
fruit in the forest.*

The Dhammapada

*Sufferings increase like the abounding Birana
grass for whomever this fierce thirst overcomes.*

*Sufferings will fall, like water drops from a lotus
leaf, from the one who overcomes this fierce thirst, so
difficult to overcome in this world.*

*Dig up the root of craving, as one who wants
the sweet scented Ushira root must dig up the root of
the Birana grass. That way, Mara, the tempter, will
not be able to crush you again and again, as the
stream crushes the reeds.*

*As a tree is firm as long as its root is safe and
grows again even though it has been cut down, so it is
with craving. Unless you destroy the very root of
craving, this pain of life will return again and again.*

*One whose desire for pleasure runs strong in the
thirty-six channels will be carried away by the wave of
his passions.*

*The channels of pleasure run everywhere.
The creeper of passion stands sprouting. If you see
the creeper springing up, then cut its root by means
of knowledge.*

*A creature's pleasures are extravagant and
luxurious. Sunk in the bog of craving and looking for
pleasure, people undergo, again and again, birth and
decay.*

The Dhammapada

People, driven by craving, run around like a snared hare. Held in fetters and bonds they undergo suffering for a long time, again and again.

You, who have come out of the pit of the hell-state, are you foolish enough to rush back into the pit?

Wise people do not call something a strong fetter that is made of iron, wood or hemp. Far stronger is the fetter of desire for precious stones, wealth and a family.

Wise people call that fetter strong which drags down, yields, but is difficult to undo. After having cut this fetter of craving and leaving desires and pleasures behind at last, people enter upon the Path, free from cares.

Those who are slaves to passions run up and down the stream of desires, as a spider runs up and down the web, which he himself has created.

Give up what is before, give up what is behind, and give up what is in between. When you go to the other shore of existence, if your mind is altogether free, you will not again enter into birth and decay.

If someone is tossed about by doubts, full of strong passions and yearns only for what is delightful, then his thirst will grow more and more, and he will indeed make his fetters strong.

The Dhammapada

If someone delights in quieting doubts and, always reflecting, thinks about what is beneficial, he will not only remove but also cut the fetters of Mara, the tempter.

The one who has reached the end of the journey, who does not tremble, who is without craving and without desire, has broken all the thorns of life. This will be his last body.

One who is without thirst and without passion, who understands the Teaching and knows the reality of all things, has received his last body. He is a great sage.

I have conquered all. I know all. In all conditions of life I am free from taint. I have left all, and through the destruction of craving I am free.

The gift of the Law is the greatest of gifts, the sweetness of the Law is the greatest sweetness, the delight of the Law is the greatest delight, and the extinction of craving overcomes all suffering.

Wealth destroys the foolish, if they are not looking for the other shore. The fool, by his thirst for wealth, destroys himself, as if he were his own worst enemy.

The fields are damaged by weeds. Mankind is damaged by passion. Therefore, a gift bestowed on those who are free from passion brings great reward.

The Dhammapada

The fields are damaged by weeds. Mankind is damaged by hatred. Therefore, a gift bestowed on those who do not hate brings great reward.

The fields are damaged by weeds. Mankind is damaged by vanity. Therefore, a gift bestowed on those who are free from vanity brings great reward.

The fields are damaged by weeds. Mankind is damaged by craving. Therefore, a gift bestowed on those who are free from craving brings great reward.

The Bhikshu (The Seeker)

Restraint of the sight is good, as is restraint of the ear. Restraint of the sense of smell is good, and it is good to restrain the tongue.

Restraint of the body is good, as is restraint of the speech and mind. A Bhikshu, restrained in all things, is freed from all sufferings.

The one who controls his body, who delights inwardly, who is undisturbed and content, is one people call a Bhikshu.

The words are sweet coming from the Bhikshu who controls his speech, speaks wisely and calmly, and speaks of the Law.

The Dhammapada

The Bhikshu who dwells in the Law, delights in the Law, and follows the Law will never fall away from the True Law.

Let no one take for granted the talents he has received and envy the talents of others. A person who envies others will never obtain peace of mind for himself.

Even the heavenly beings will praise the Bhikshu who, though he possesses little, does not take his talents for granted, is pure and is not lazy.

One is indeed a Bhikshu who does not identify himself with his body and who does not grieve over the past.

The Bhikshu who acts with compassion, who is knowledgeable in the dharma of the Buddha and has lost all desires will reach Nirvana, the highest happiness.

Empty your boat, O seeker! After cutting off craving and hatred it will sail quickly into Nirvana.

Cut off the five hindrances! A Bhikshu who has escaped from the five fetters is called, 'One who is saved from the flood.'

Meditate and do not be thoughtless! Do not direct your thoughts toward pleasure! In this way you will avoid having to swallow the red-hot ball of hell.

The Dhammapada

Without wisdom there is no meditation, and without meditation there is no wisdom. One who has wisdom and meditates is near Nirvana.

A Bhikshu, who has emptied his mind and whose mind is tranquil, feels delight after seeing the Path clearly.

As soon as the Bhikshu has considered the origin and destruction of the elements of the body, he finds the happiness and joy which belong to those who know the Immortal.

It is wise for a Bhikshu to restrain his senses, be content, and keep noble friends who are not lazy.

Let the noble ones give charitably; let them be perfect in their duties. In this way, they will end all suffering.

Bhikshu, as the Vassika plant sheds its withered flowers, so should you shed all passions and hatred!

One whose body, mind and tongue have been quieted, who is calm and collected, and who has rejected all the temptations of the world, is indeed called a 'Bhikshu.'

The Dhammapada

Rouse yourself! Do not be idle! Examine yourself and be attentive! In this way you will live happily.

Self is the master of Self. Self is the refuge of Self. Therefore, tame your Self as the merchant tames a good horse.

The Bhikshu, who is comfortable and full of delight in the doctrine of the Buddha, will reach the quiet place which is called Nirvana and will brighten up this world, like the moon when freed from the clouds.

Stop the stream valiantly; drive away all desires, O Bhikshu! When you have understood the destruction of all that was made, you will understand that which was not made.

If the Bhikshu has reached the other shore in both the laws of restraint and contemplation, then all bonds will vanish from this one who has obtained wisdom.

The Brahmana (The Enlightened)

One for whom there is neither this nor the other shore, the fearless and unshackled, I indeed call a Brahmana.

The Dhammapada

One who is thoughtful, blameless, settled, dutiful, without passions, and who has attained Nirvana, I indeed call a Brahmana.

The sun is bright by day, and the moon is bright by night. The warrior is bright in his armor. The Bhikshu is bright in his meditation, and the Enlightened are bright with splendor day and night.

No one should attack a Brahmana, but no Brahmana, if attacked, should let himself fly at his aggressor! Woe to the one who strikes a Brahmana, but more woe to the Brahmana who shows anger toward his aggressor!

It advantages a Brahmana to hold his mind back from the pleasures of this world. When all desire to injure has vanished, your pain and suffering will cease.

One I indeed call a Brahmana who does not offend by body, word or thought, and is controlled on these three points.

After someone has understood the Law as taught by the Awakened One, let him worship it carefully, as the Brahmana worships the sacrificial fire.

A person does not become a Brahmana by his platted hair or by his family connections. One in whom there is truth and righteousness can be called a Brahmana.

What is the use of platted hair and clothing made of goatskins? There is cleanliness on the outside, but the inside is like ravenous wolves.

One who wears dirty clothing, who is emaciated and covered with veins, if his thoughts are pure and he meditates, will be called a Brahmana.

I do not call someone a Brahmana because of his origin or his family. He may be wealthy and called 'Sir' by others, but the poor who are free from all attachments and free from craving; those I call Brahmanas.

One who has cut all fetters and who never trembles, who is independent and unshackled, I indeed call a Brahmana.

One who has cut the girdle and the strap, the rope with all that pertains to it, who has burst the bar and is awakened, I indeed call a Brahmana.

One who, although he commits no offense, endures reproach and who is strong and powerful in endurance, I indeed call a Brahmana.

One who is free from anger, dutiful, virtuous, without weakness, humble and who has received his last body, I indeed call a Brahmana.

The Dhammapada

One who does not cling to pleasure, from whom pleasure drops off like water from a lotus leaf, I indeed call a Brahmana.

One who, even in this life, knows the end of suffering, has put down the burden of craving and is unshackled, I indeed call a Brahmana.

One whose knowledge of the Law is deep, who possesses wisdom, who knows between right and wrong and who has attained Nirvana, I indeed call a Brahmana.

One who is detached from this world and whose desires are extinguished, I indeed call a Brahmana.

One who does not judge or find fault with others, who does not kill or cause the slaughter of either human beings or animals, I indeed call a Brahmana.

One who is tolerant with the intolerant, without judgement among those who judge and free from passion among the passionate, I indeed call a Brahmana.

One from whom anger and hatred, pride and envy have dropped off like a mustard seed from the point of a needle, I indeed call a Brahmana.

One who speaks the truth, whose speech is instructive, innofensive and free from harshness, I indeed call a Brahmana.

The Dhammapada

One who takes nothing in the world that is not given to him, I indeed call a Brahmana.

One who fosters no desires for this world or the next, has no attachments and is unshackled, I indeed call a Brahmana.

One who has no interest in this world and when he has understood the Truth does not ask, 'How?', and can dive into the Immortal, I indeed call a Brahmana.

One who has risen above both good and evil and who is free from grief, sin and impurity, I indeed call a Brahmana.

One who is bright like the moon, pure, serene and undisturbed, I indeed call a Brahmana.

One who has traversed this mazy, impervious world and all its vanity, who has reached the other shore, is thoughtful, guileless, free from doubts, free from attachments and who is content, I indeed call a Brahmana.

One who, after leaving all desires behind, travels about without a home and in whom all concupiscence is extinct, I indeed call a Brahmana.

One who, after being freed from the bondage of craving, has risen above all desires and who is free from the five hindrances, I indeed call a Brahmana.

The Dhammapada

One who has left both pleasure and pain, who is free from the germs of renewed life, the hero who has conquered the world, I indeed call a Brahmana.

One who knows about the destruction and return of creatures everywhere, who is free from the five fetters and is awake, I indeed call a Brahmana.

One whose path is undetectable and whose passions are extinct, I indeed call a Brahmana.

One who calls nothing his own, whether it be before, behind or in between, who is poor and free from the love of this world, I indeed call a Brahmana.

The noble, the hero, the great sage, the conqueror, the guileless, the master, the awakened, I indeed call a Brahmana.

One who sees the flow of his many lives, who understands what the suffering of hell is and what is the perfect joy of heaven, who has reached the end of births and has attained Nirvana, I indeed call a Brahmana.

The Diamond Sutra

The Diamond Sutra

Thus I have heard. Once the Buddha was traveling in the kingdom of Shravasti, staying in the Jetavana Grove, and assembled there with him were twelve hundred and fifty experienced Bodhisattvas. As the hour drew near for the morning meal the Buddha and his disciples put on their street robes and, carrying their alms bowls, went toward the city of Shravasti and begged door to door for their food. After they had returned to the Jeta Grove they laid aside their street garments, washed their feet, partook of the morning meal, put away their begging bowls for another day, and afterward seated themselves before the Buddha.

The venerable Subhuti rose from his seat in the middle of the assembly, arranged his robes so that his right shoulder was exposed, kneeled on his right knee, pressed the palms of his hands together and, bowing respectfully to the Buddha, said, "Tathagata, World-honored One, may your mercy be upon us to take good care of us and to give us your good instruction!"

The Buddha replied to Subhuti saying, *"Indeed, I will take good care of every Bodhisattva-Mahasattva and give them the best of instruction!"*

The Diamond Sutra

Subhuti said to the Buddha, "World-honored One! We are delighted to listen to your blessed instruction. Tell us what we shall say when good worthy men and women come to us inquiring how they should begin the practice of seeking to attain Enlightenment. What shall we tell them? How are they to quiet their drifting minds and subdue their craving thoughts?"

The Buddha replied to Subhuti, "*You have made a good request, Subhuti. Listen carefully and I will answer your question so that all the Bodhisattvas will understand. When good and worthy men and women come to you wishing to begin the practice of seeking to attain Enlightenment they will simply have to follow what I am about to say to you, and very soon they will be able to subdue their craving desires and discriminative thoughts, and will be able to attain perfect tranquility of mind.*"

Then the Buddha addressed the assembly saying, "*Everyone in the world, beginning with the highest Bodhisattva should follow what I am going to teach you. This teaching will bring deliverance to everyone whether hatched from an egg, formed in a womb, evolved from spawn, or produced by metamorphosis with or without form, possessing mental faculties or*

The Diamond Sutra

*devoid of mental faculties, and lead them toward
Perfect Enlightenment. Though the sentient beings
still to be delivered to me are innumerable and without
limit yet, in reality, there are no sentient beings to be
delivered. And why, Subhuti? It is because should there
exist in the minds of Bodhisattva-Mahasattvas such
arbitrary conceptions of phenomena as the existence of
one's own Ego-Selfness, the Ego-Selfness of another or
the Ego-Selfness as divided into an infinite number of
living and dying beings, they would be unworthy to be
called Bodhisattva-Mahasattvas. Moreover, Subhuti,
the Bodhisattva-Mahasattvas, in teaching the Dharma
to others, should first be free themselves from all the
craving thoughts awakened by beautiful sights, pleasant sounds, sweet tastes, soft tangibles, fragrances,
and seductive thoughts. In their practice of charity,
they should not be influenced by any of these seductive
phenomena. Why? It is because if, in their practice of
charity, such things do not influence them, then they
will realize a blessing and merit that is inestimable and
inconceivable. What do you think, Subhuti? Is it possible to estimate the distance of space in the eastern,
northern, southern and western heavens, or to any of
the four corners of the universe?"* Subhuti replied,
"No, World-honored One! It is not possible to

estimate the distance of space in the heavens or the universe." The Buddha continued, "*Subhuti, it is equally impossible to estimate the blessing and merit that will come to the Bodhisattva-Mahasattva who practices charity uninfluenced by any of these arbitrary conceptions of seductive phenomena. What do you think, Subhuti? If a disciple should bestow as alms an abundance of the seven treasures sufficient to fill the three thousand fold worlds would he thereby acquire a considerable blessing and merit?*" Subhuti replied, "World-honored One! Such a disciple would acquire a very considerable blessing!"

The Buddha said, "*Subhuti, if any good and pious disciple, man or woman, for the sake of charity has been sacrificing his or her life for generation after generation and another disciple has been simply studying and observing even one stanza of this Sutra and explaining it to others, his blessing and merit will be far greater. When a disciple begins the practice of attaining Supreme Enlightenment he must also give up all clinging to arbitrary conceptions about phenomena. When engaged in thinking, he should definitely exclude all thoughts connected with the phenomena of sight, sound, taste, smell, touch, and all discriminations based upon them, keeping his thinking independent of*

*all such arbitrary conceptions of phenomena. The mind
is disturbed by these discriminations of sense concepts
and, as the mind becomes disturbed, it falls into false
imaginations as to one's Self and its relation to other
Selves. It is for this reason that the Tathagata has
constantly urged the Bodhisattva-Mahasattvas in their
practice of charity not to be influenced by any arbitrary
conceptions of sight, sound, taste, smell, touch, and all
discriminations based upon them.*

*The Bodhisattva-Mahasattvas should also give
alms, uninfluenced by any preconceived thoughts as to
Self and other Selves and for the sole purpose of bene-
fiting sentient beings, always remembering that both
the phenomena and sentient beings are to be considered
as mere expressions. Nevertheless, Subhuti, the teaching
of the Tathagata is true, credible, immutable; it is
neither extravagant nor imaginary. The same is true
of the attainments of the Tathagatas; they should be
considered as neither realities nor as unrealities.
Subhuti, if a Bodhisattva-Mahasattva, in practicing
charity, conceives within his mind any of these conceptions discriminating his Self from other Selves, he
will be like a person walking in darkness and seeing
nothing. But if the Bodhisattva-Mahasattva, in his
practice of charity, has no conceptions in regards to*

his Self or other Selves, then he will be like a person with good eyes seeing all things clearly in the bright sunshine.

If, in future ages, there should be any good and pious disciple, either man or woman, who is able to faithfully observe and study this Sutra, his attainment of inestimable and illimitable blessing and merit will be instantly known and appreciated by the Transcendental Eye of the Tathagata."

The Buddha continued, "Subhuti, when a disciple is moved to make objective gifts of charity, he should also practice the Sila Paramita of selfless kindness. He should remember that there is no arbitrary distinction between one's own Self and the Selfhood of others. Therefore, he should practice charity by giving not only objective gifts, but also the selfless gifts of kindness and sympathy. If any disciple will simply practice kindness, he will soon attain Enlightenment.

Subhuti, if any disciple added together the seven treasures forming an elevation as high as Mount Sumeru and donated them to charity, his merit would still be less than the merit of the disciple who simply observed and studied this Sutra and from the kindness of his heart explained it to others. That disciple would accumulate a greater blessing by a hundred to one, *even a hundred thousand myriads to one.*

Do not think, Subhuti, that the Tathagata would consider within himself, 'I will deliver sentient beings.' Why? It is because really there are no sentient beings to be delivered by the Tathagata. Should there be any sentient beings to be delivered by the Tathagata, it would mean that the Tathagata was cherishing within his mind arbitrary conceptions of phenomena such as one's own Self and other Selves. Even when the Tathagata refers to himself, he is not holding in his mind any such arbitrary thought. Only earthly human beings think of Selfhood as being a personal possession. Subhuti, even the expression 'earthly beings' as used by the Tathagata does not mean that there are any such beings. It is only a figure of speech. Subhuti, if a disciple bestowed as alms an abundance of treasures sufficient to fill as many worlds as there are grains of sand in the Ganges river, and if another disciple, having realized the Truth of the ego-lessness of all things and thereby had attained perfect selflessness, that selfless disciple would have more blessing and merit than the one who merely practiced objective charity. Any why? It is because those blessings and merit were never sought with a covetous spirit by the Bodhisattva, so by that same spirit he does not look

*upon them as a private possession, but as the common
possession of all sentient beings."*

The Buddha continued, *"What do you think,
Subhuti? Suppose a disciple has attained the stage of
Crotapanna. Could this disciple make any kind of
arbitrary assertion such as, 'I have entered the
stream'?"* Subhuti replied, "No, World-honored
One! Because, while, by that measure of attainment, it means that he has entered the Holy
Stream, yet, speaking truly, he has not entered
anything, nor has his mind entertained any
arbitrary concepts such as form, sound, taste,
odor, touch and discrimination. It is because of
that degree of attainment that he is entitled to be
called Crotapanna."

The Buddha asked, *"What do you think,
Subhuti? Suppose a disciple has attained the stage
of Sakradagamin. Could he make any such arbitrary
assertion as, 'I have attained the stage of one more
return'?"* Subhuti answered, "No, World-honored
One! Because by the stage of Sakradagamin it is
meant that he is to be reborn but once more.
Yet, speaking truly, there will be no rebirth. It
is because he knows this that he is to be called
Sakradagamin."

The Diamond Sutra

The Buddha asked, *"What do you think, Subhuti? Suppose a disciple has attained the stage of Anagamin. Could he hold within his mind any such arbitrary conception as, 'I have attained the stage of never to return'?"* Subhuti answered, "No, World-honored One! Because by the stage of Anagamin it means that he is never to return, yet, speaking truthfully, one who has reached that stage never cherishes any such arbitrary conception. It is for this reason that he is entitled to be called Anagamin."

The Buddha asked, *"What do you think, Subhuti? Suppose a disciple has attained the stage of Arahat. Could he entertain within his mind any such arbitrary conception as, 'I have become fully enlightened'?"* Subhuti replied, "No, World-honored One! Because, speaking truthfully, there is no such thing as a fully enlightened one. Should a disciple who has attained such a degree of enlightenment cherish within his mind, 'I have become fully enlightened,' he would soon be grasping after such things as his own Selfhood and the Selfhood of others."

The Buddha asked, *"What do you think, Subhuti? Do the Bodhisattva-Mahasattvas embellish*

the *Buddha-lands to which they go?"* Subhuti said,
"No, World-honored One! Because what is
meant by the expression 'embellishment of
the Buddha-lands' is self-contradictory, since
Buddha-lands thus embellished could no longer
be called Buddha-lands. Therefore, the expression 'embellishments of the Buddha-lands' is
merely a figure of speech." The Buddha said,
*"It is for this reason, Subhuti, that the minds of all
Bodhisattvas should be purified of all conceptions
related to seeing, hearing, tasting, smelling, touching,
and discriminating. They should use their mental
faculties spontaneously and naturally, unconstrained
by any preconceptions arising from the senses. Subhuti,
should there be among the disciples some who have not
yet purified their karma and who must first suffer the
natural retribution of wrongs committed in some
previous life, and should they earnestly and faithfully
observe and study this Sutra, then their karma will
immediately become purified and they will at once
attain Perfect Enlightenment.*

*Subhuti, I recall that long ago, numberless myriads
of kalpas ago, I served and worshipped with offerings
and received spiritual instruction and discipline from
eight hundred and four thousand myriads of Buddhas,*

yet in the far off ages of the last kalpa of this world, if a disciple shall faithfully observe, study and put into practice the teachings of this Sutra, then the blessings he will gain will far exceed that which was aquired by me during those long years of service and discipline under those many Buddhas. Subhuti, in contrast to what I have said about the inestimable blessings that will come to earnest disciples who observe, study and practice this Sutra in that far off last kalpa, I must tell you that there will be some disciples who, upon hearing this Sutra, will become bewildered in their minds and will not believe it. Subhuti, you should remember that just as the teaching of this Sutra transcends human thought, so the effect and the final result of studying it and putting it into practice is also inscrutable."

The Buddha said, *"What do you think, Subhuti? If there are as many Ganges rivers as there are grains of sand in the river Ganges, will these rivers be very numerous?"* Subhuti answered, "Exceedingly numerous, Blessed One!" The Buddha replied, *"Supposing that these innumerable rivers existed, how immeasurable would be their grains of sand! Subhuti, if a good and pious disciple, man or woman, should give as alms an amount of the seven treasures equal to those grains of sand, would the merit that he accrues* be a considerable amount?" Subhuti answered, "A very considerable amount indeed, Blessed One!" The Buddha said, *"Subhuti, if another disciple after studying and observing even one stanza of this Sutra should explain it to others, then his blessing and merit would be greater. Moreover, Subhuti, if any disciple in any place should teach even one stanza of this Sutra to others, then that place will become sacred ground to which countless divas and angels will bring offerings. Such places, however humble they may be, will be reverenced as though they were famous temples and pagodas, to which countless pilgrims will come to offer worship and incense. And divas and angels will hover over them like a cloud, and will sprinkle an offering of celestial flowers upon them. How much more sacred would that place become if a disciple studied and observed the entire Sutra! Rest assured, Subhuti, that such a disciple would surely succeed in the attainment of Enlightenment, and the place where this Sutra is reverenced will be like an altar consecrated to the Buddha.*

Subhuti, should there be any good and pious disciple, man or woman, who in his zeal to practice charity is willing to sacrifice his life morning, noon and night, would his blessing and merit be great?" Subhuti

108

replied, "It would be very great indeed, Blessed One." The Buddha said, "*Suppose, Subhuti, that another disciple observes and studies this Sutra in pure faith. His blessing and merit would be greater. And if still another disciple, besides observing and studying this Sutra, zealously explains it to others, copies and circulates it, his blessing and merit would be even greater. In others words, Subhuti, this Sutra is invested with a virtue and power that is inestimable, illimitable and indescribable. The Tathagata reveals this Sutra only to those disciples who are earnestly and perseveringly seeking the perfect realization of Nirvana. As disciples become able to zealously and faithfully observe and study this Sutra, explain it to others and circulate it widely, the Tathagata will recognize and support them until they succeed. Such disciples will share with the Tathagata its burden of compassion and its reward of Nirvana.*" Then Subhuti inquired of the Buddha, saying, "Suppose a good and pious disciple, either man or woman, having begun the practice of attaining Supreme Enlightenment, still finds his mind to be disturbed. How is he to keep his mind tranquil? How is he to wholly subdue his wandering thoughts and craving desires?" The Buddha replied, "*Subhuti, any good* and pious disciple who understands the practice of concentrating his mind in an effort to realize Supreme Enlightenment should cherish only one thought, namely, 'when I attain this highest Perfect Wisdom, I will bring all sentient beings into the eternal peace of Nirvana.' If this purpose and vow is sincere, then these sentient beings are already delivered. And yet, Subhuti, if the full truth were told, one would know that not a single sentient being has ever been delivered. Why, Subhuti? It is because if the Bodhisattva-Mahasattvas have kept in mind any such arbitrary conceptions as one's own Self or the Selfhood of others, then they could not be called Bodhisattva-Mahasattvas. And what does this mean, Subhuti? It means that there are no sentient beings to be delivered and there is no Selfhood that can begin the practice of seeking to attain Perfect Enlightenment. It means that what I attained is not something limited and arbitrary that can be called 'Perfect Enlightenment', but is Buddhahood, whose essence is identical with the essence of all things and it is what it is - universal, inconceivable and inscrutable."

The Buddha said, "Subhuti, the Buddhahood to which the Tathagata has attained is both the same as 'Perfect Enlightenment' and it is not the same. This is only another way of saying that the phenomena of all

The Diamond Sutra

things are One with Buddhahood and Nirvana, and that it is neither reality nor unreality. It abides together with all phenomena in emptiness and silence; inconceivable and inscrutable. Subhuti, that is why I say that the Dharma of all things can never be embraced within any arbitrary conception of phenomena however universal that conception may be. That is why it is called the Dharma and why there is no such thing as the Dharma."

The Buddha asked, *"Subhuti, What do you think? Does the Tathagata possess a physical eye?"* Subhuti replied, "Surely, Blessed One, He possesses a physical eye." The Buddha asked Subhuti, *"Does He possess the Eye of Enlightenment?"* Subhuti said, "Certainly the Tathagata possesses the Eye of Enlightenment; otherwise he would not be the Buddha." The Buddha asked, *"Does the Tathagata possess the Eye of Transcendental Intelligence?"* Subhuti said, "Yes, Blessed One, the Tathagata definitely possesses the Eye of Transcendental Intelligence." The Buddha asked, *"Does the Tathagata possess the Eye of Spiritual Intuition?"* Subhuti answered, "Yes, Blessed One, the Tathagata most certainly possesses the Eye of Spiritual Intuition." The Buddha asked Subhuti,

The Diamond Sutra

"Does the Tathagata possess the eye of a Buddha's love and compassion for all sentient life?" Subhuti replied, "World-honored One! We know that you love all sentient life." The Buddha said, "What do you think, Subhuti? When I referred to the grains of sand in the river Ganges, did I assert that they were truly grains of sand?" Subhuti said, "No, Blessed One, you only spoke of them as grains of sand." The Buddha said, "Subhuti, if there were as many Ganges rivers as there are grains of sand in the river Ganges, and if there were as many Buddha-lands as there are grains of sand in all of these innumerable rivers, would these Buddha-lands be considered as being very numerous?" Subhuti replied, "Very numerous indeed, Bessed One!" Then the Buddha said, "Listen carefully, Subhuti. Within these innumerable Buddha-lands there are every form of sentient beings with all of their various mentalities and conceptions, all of which are fully known to the Tathagata, but not one of them is held in the Tathagata's mind as an arbitrary conception of phenomena. They are merely thoughts. Not even one of these vast accumulations of conceptions from beginning-less time, through the present and into the never-ending future, is capable of being grasped. Subhuti, if any good and pious *disciple, either man or woman, were to take the three thousand great universes and grind them to powder and blow that powder into space, would this powder have any individual existence?"* Subhuti replied, "Yes, Blessed One, as a powder infinitely dissipated, it might be said to have a relative existence, but as the Blessed One uses the words, it has no existence. The words have only a figurative meaning; otherwise the words would imply a belief in the existence of matter as an independent and Self-existent entity, which it is not. Moreover, when the Tathagata refers to the 'three thousand great universes,' he could only do so as a figure of speech because if the three thousand great universes really existed, then their only reality would consist in their cosmic unity. What does it matter whether they are in the form of powder or three thousand great universes? It is only in the sense of the cosmic unity of ultimate essence that the Tathagata can rightfully refer to it." The Buddha was very much pleased with this reply and said, *"Subhuti, although earthly human beings have always tried to understand the conception of matter and great universes, the conception has no reality – it is an illusion of mortal mind. Even when it is referred to as 'cosmic unity' it is something that cannot be understood.*

If any disciple were to say that the Tathagata, in his teachings, has constantly referred to HimSelf or other Selves would that disciple have understood the meaning of what I have been teaching?" Subhuti replied, "No, Blessed One! That disciple would not have understood the meaning of the Buddha's teachings, because when the Buddha has referred to them he has never referred to their actual existence. He has only used the words as figures of speech. It is only in that sense that they can be used because conceptions, ideas, limited truths and Dharma have no more reality than have matter and phenomena." The Buddha emphasized this, saying, *"Subhuti, when disciples begin their practice of seeking to attain Perfect Enlightenment, they ought to see, perceive, know, understand and realize that all things are no-things, and, therefore, they should not conceive within their minds any arbitrary conceptions whatsoever about them. Subhuti, how is it possible to explain this Sutra to others without holding in one's mind any arbitrary conceptions of phenomena and Dharma? It can only be done by keeping the mind in perfect tranquility and in selfless Oneness that is Tathagatahood. Why, Subhuti? It is because all of the mind's arbitrary conceptions of matter, phenomena and ideas relating to them are like a dream, a bubble, a shadow, evanescent dew, or the lightning's flash. Every true disciple should therefore keep his mind empty, selfless and tranquil."*

The Buddha said, *"What do you think, Subhuti? Has the Tathagata attained to anything that can be described as Perfect Enlightenment? Has he ever given you any such teaching?"* Subhuti replied, "As I understand the teaching, there is no such thing as Perfect Enlightenment nor is it possible for the Tathagata to teach any fixed Dharma. Why? It is because the things taught by the Tathagata are, in their essential nature, inconceivable and impossible to understand; they are neither existent nor non-existent. It means that Bodhisattvas are not enlightened by fixed teachings but rather by an intuitive process that is spontaneous and natural."

Then Subhuti respectfully asked the Buddha, "World-honored One! In future days, if a disciple hears this teaching or a part of it, will it awaken true faith in his mind?" The Buddha replied, *"Subhuti, do not doubt it. Even at the remote period of*

*five hundred years after the Nirvana of the Tathagata,
there will be those who, practicing charity and keeping
the precepts, will believe in sections and sentences of
this Sutra and will awaken within their minds a true
pure faith. Subhuti, the Tathagata knows that the
sentient beings who awaken faith after hearing
sentences and sections of this Sutra will accumulate an
inestimable blessing and merit. How do I know this? It
is because these sentient beings have already discarded
such arbitrary conceptions of phenomena, as one's own
Self and the Selfhood of others. If they had not, then
their minds would inevitably grasp after such things,
and then they would not be able to practice charity nor
keep the precepts. Moreover, these sentient beings must
have also discarded all arbitrary ideas relating to the
conceptions of a personal Self or other Selves. If they
had not, then their minds would inevitably grasp after
such relative ideas. Furthermore, these sentient beings
must have already discarded all arbitrary ideas relating
to the conception of the non-existence of a personal Self
or other Selves. If they had not, then their minds would
still be grasping after such ideas. Therefore, every disciple who is seeking after enlightenment should discard,
not only conceptions of one's own Selfhood and the
Selfhood of others, but should also discard all ideas*

The Diamond Sutra

about such conceptions and all ideas about the non-existence of such conceptions. While the Tathagata, in his teaching, constantly makes use of conceptions and ideas about them, disciples should keep in mind the unreality of all such conceptions and ideas. They should remember that the Tathagata, in making use of them in explaining the Dharma, always uses them in the resemblance of a raft that is only used to cross a river. As the raft is of no further use after the river is crossed, it should be discarded. Likewise, these arbitrary conceptions of existent and non-existent phenomena should be given up as one attains enlightenment."

As Subhuti listened intently to the Buddha's words, the teaching of this Sutra penetrated into the depths of his understanding and he fully realized that it was the true Path to Enlightenment. The tears came to his eyes as he realized this and he said, "World-honored One! I have never before realized this profound Sutra. You have opened my eyes to its Transcendendal Wisdom. World-honored One! By what name shall this Sutra be known, so that it will be understood and honored and studied?" The Buddha replied, *"This Sutra shall be known as the Vajracchedika Prajna Paramita. By this name it shall be reverenced,*

*studied and observed. What is meant by this name? It
means that when the Buddha named it Prajna Paramita, he did not have in mind any definite or arbitrary
conception and so he thus named it. It is the Sutra
that is hard and sharp like a diamond that will cut
away all arbitrary conceptions, and bring one to the
other shore of Enlightenment. What do you think,
Subhuti? Has the Tathagata given you any definite
teaching in this Sutra?"* Subhuti replied, "No,
Blessed One! The Tathagata has not given us
any definite teaching in this Sutra."

When the Buddha had finished the teaching
recorded in this Sutra, the venerable Subhuti,
together with all the assembled Bodhisattva-
Mahavattvas greatly rejoiced and, sincerely believing the teaching, they heartily accepted it,
faithfully observed it, and zealously practiced it.

The Sutra
of
Innumerable Meanings

The Sutra of Innumerable Meanings

Thus I have heard. Once the Buddha was staying at the City of Royal Palaces on Mount Grdhrakuta with a great assemblage of great bhikshus, in all twelve thousand. There were eighty thousand bodhisattvas. There were heavenly beings, dragons, yakshas, gandharvas, asuras, garudas, kimnaras and mahorages, besides all the bhikshus, bhikshunis, upasakas and upasikas. There were great wheel-rolling kings, small wheel-rolling kings, and kings of the gold wheel, silver wheel and other wheels. Further, there were kings and princes, ministers, men and women, and great rich persons, each accompanied by a hundred thousand myriad followers.

They went up to the Buddha, made obeisance at his feet, made processions around him, burned incense and scattered flowers. After they variously worshiped, they retired and sat to one side. Of all these bodhisattvas there is none who is not a great saint of the Law. They have attained commands, meditations, wisdom, emancipation and the knowledge of emancipation. With tranquil minds and constantly in contemplation, they are peaceful, indifferent, non-active and free from desires. They are immune from any kind of delusion or distraction. Their minds are calm and clear, profound and infinite. Having obtained the great wisdom, they penetrate all things, completely understand the reality of their nature and form, and clearly discriminate existing and nonexisting, long and short.

The eighty thousand bodhisattvas in the assembly made obeisance at the Buddha's feet, made processions around him, burned celestial incense, scattered celestial flowers and presented the Buddha with celestial robes, garlands and jewels. They placed celestial banners, flags, canopies and playthings everywhere, pleased the Buddha with celestial music, then went forth to kneel with folded hands and praised him in verse.

At that time the Bodhisattva Great Adornment, along with the eighty thousand bodhisattvas, finished praising the Buddha and said to the Buddha in unison, "World-honored One! We, the assemblage of the eighty thousand bodhisattvas want to ask you about the Tathagata's Law. We are anxious that the World-honored One would hear us with sympathy."

The Buddha addressed the Bodhisattva Great

Adornment and the eighty thousand bodhisattvas, *"Excellent! Excellent! Good sons and daughters,
you have well known that this is the time. Ask me
whatever you like. Before long the Tathagata will enter
parinirvana. After nirvana, there shall not be a doubt
left to anybody. I will answer any question you wish to
ask."*

Thereupon the Bodhisattva Great Adornment, with the eighty thousand bodhisattvas,
said to the Buddha in unison and with one voice,
"World-honored One! If the bodhisattvas want
to accomplish Perfect Enlightenment quickly,
what doctrine should they practice? What doctrine makes bodhisattvas accomplish Perfect
Enlightenment quickly?"

The Buddha addressed the eighty thousand
bodhisattvas, *"Good sons and daughters! There is one
doctrine that makes bodhisattvas accomplish Perfect
Enlightenment quickly. If a bodhisattva learns this
doctrine, then they will accomplish Perfect Enlightenment quickly."*

The Bodhisattva Great Adornment replied,
"World-honored One! What is this doctrine
called? What is its meaning? How does a bodhisattva practice it?"

123

The Sutra of Innumerable Meanings

The Buddha answered them saying, "Good sons and daughters! This one doctrine is called the Sutra of Innumerable Meanings. A bodhisattva, if he wants to learn and master the Sutra of Innumerable Meanings, should observe that all laws, or existences, were originally, will be, and are in themselves void in nature and form. They are neither great nor small, neither appearing nor disappearing, neither fixed nor movable, neither advancing nor retreating, and they are non-dualistic, just emptiness. All living beings, however, discriminate falsely, 'It is this' or 'It is that', and 'It is advantageous' or 'It is disadvantageous.' They entertain evil thoughts, make various evil karmas, and thus transmigrate within the six realms of existence, and they suffer all manner of miseries and cannot escape from there during infinite kotis of kalpas. Bodhisattvas, observing rightly like this, should raise the mind of compassion, display the great mercy desiring to relieve others of suffering, and once again penetrate deeply into all laws.

According to the nature of a law, such a law, or existence, emerges. According to the nature of a law, such a law settles. According to the nature of a law, such a law changes. According to the nature of a law, such a law vanishes. According to the nature of a law, such an evil law emerges. According to the nature of a law, such a good law emerges. Settling, changing and vanishing are also like this.

Bodhisattvas, having completely observed and known these four aspects from beginning to end, should next observe that none of the laws, or existences, settles down even for a moment, and observe that they emerge, settle, change and vanish instantly. After such observations, we see all manner of natural desires of living beings. As natural desires are innumerable, preaching is immeasurable, and as preaching is immeasurable, meanings are innumerable.

The innumerable meanings originate from one law. This one law is, namely, non-form. Such non-form is formless, and not form. Being not form and formless, it is called the Real Aspect of things.

The mercy which bodhisattvas display after stabilizing themselves in such a real aspect is real and not in vain. They excellently relieve living beings from sufferings. Having given relief from sufferings, they preach the Law again and let all living beings obtain pleasure.

Good sons and daughters! A bodhisattva, if he practices completely the doctrine of the Sutra of Innumerable Meanings like this, will soon accomplish Perfect Enlightenment without fail.

The Sutra of Innumerable Meanings

The Sutra of Innumerable Meanings, such a profound and supreme Great-vehicle, is reasonable in its logic, unsurpassed in its worth, and protected by all the Buddhas of the three worlds. No kind of demon or heretic can break into it, nor can any wrong view of life and death destroy it. Therefore, bodhisattvas, if you want to accomplish supreme Buddhahood quickly, you should learn and master the Sutra of Innumerable Meanings, such a profound and supreme Great-vehicle."

At that time the Bodhisattva Great Adornment said to the Buddha, "World-honored One! This sutra is inconceivable. World-honored One! Be pleased to explain the profound and inconceivable matter of this sutra out of benevolence for all the people. World-honored One! From what place does this sutra come? For what place does it leave? At what place does it stay? Whereupon does this sutra make people accomplish Perfect Enlightenment, having such infinite powers?"

At that time the Buddha addressed the Bodhisattva Great Adornment, *"Excellent! Excellent! Good son, just so, just so, just as you say. I preach this sutra as profound, profound, and truly profound.*

The Sutra of Innumerable Meanings

Wherefore? Because it makes people quickly accomplish Supreme Enlightenment. Hearing it but once is keeping all the laws; it greatly benefits all the living. There is no suffering in practicing the Great Direct Way.

Good son! You ask where this sutra comes from, where it leaves for, and where it stays. Do listen attentively. This sutra originally comes from the abode of all the Buddhas, leaves for the aspiration of all the living to Buddhahood, and stays at the place where all the bodhisattvas practice. This sutra comes like this, leaves like this, and stays like this. Therefore this sutra, having such infinite merits and inconceivable powers, makes people quickly accomplish supreme Buddhahood.

Good sons and daughters! Do you want to hear how this sutra has ten inconceivable merit-powers?"

The Bodhisattva Great Adornment said, "We heartily want to hear!"

The Buddha said, "*Good sons and daughters! First, this sutra makes the unawakened bodhisattva aspire to buddhahood, makes a merciless one raise the mind of mercy, makes a homicidal one raise the mind of great compassion, makes a jealous one raise the mind of joy, makes an attached one raise the mind of detachment, makes a miserly one raise the mind of*

The Sutra of Innumerable Meanings

donation, makes an arrogant one raise the mind of
keeping the commandments, makes an irascible one
raise the mind of assiduity, makes a distracted one
raise the mind of meditation, makes an ignorant one
raise the mind of wisdom, makes one who lacks concern for saving others raise the mind of saving others,
makes one who commits the ten evils raise the mind
of the ten virtues, makes one who has an inclination
toward apostasy raise the mind of non-retrogression,
makes one who commits defiled acts raise the mind of
purity, and makes one who suffers from delusions raise
the mind of detachment. This is called the first inconceivable merit-power of this sutra.

Good sons and daughters! Secondly, the inconceivable merit-power of this sutra is as follows: If a living
being can hear this sutra but once, or only one verse
and phrase, he will penetrate into a hundred thousand
kotis of meanings and the law kept by him cannot be
explained fully even in infinite kalpas. Wherefore? It is
because this sutra has innumerable meanings. Suppose
that from one seed a hundred thousand myriad seeds
grow. From each of a hundred thousand myriad seeds
another hundred thousand myriad seeds grow, and in
such a process seeds increase to an unlimited extent.
This sutra is like this. From one law, or existence, a

The Sutra of Innumerable Meanings

hundred thousand meanings grow and from each of a
hundred thousand meanings another hundred thousand
meanings grow, and in such a process meanings increase to an unlimited extent. Such being the case, this
sutra is called Innumerable Meanings. This is the second inconceivable merit-power of this sutra.

Good sons and daughters! Thirdly, the inconceivable merit-power of this sutra is as follows: If a living
being can hear this sutra but once, or only one verse
and phrase, he will penetrate into a hundred thousand
myriad kotis of meanings. After that, his delusions,
even though existent, will become as if nonexistent. He
will not be seized with fear, though he moves between
birth and death, and he will raise the mind of compassion for all the living and obtain the spirit of bravery
to obey the teachings. A powerful wrestler can shoulder
and hold almost any heavy thing. The keeper of this
sutra is also like this. He can shoulder the heavy treasure of supreme Buddhahood and carry living beings on
his back, out of the way of birth and death. He will be
able to relieve others from suffering, even though he
cannot yet relieve himself. Just as a ferry master,
though he stays on this shore owing to his serious illness
and unsettled body, can be made to cross over by means
of a good and solid ship that has the ability to carry

anyone without fail, so also it is with the keeper of this
sutra. Though he stays on this shore of ignorance, old
age and death, yet he can be delivered from birth and
death through practicing this strong Sutra of Innumerable Meanings as it is preached. This is called the third
inconceivable merit-power of this sutra.

Good sons and daughters! Fourthly, the inconceivable merit-power of this sutra is as follows: If a living
being can hear this sutra but once, or only one verse or
phrase, he will obtain the spirit of bravery and relieve
others from suffering, even though he cannot yet relieve
himself. He will become the attendant of the Buddhas
together with all the bodhisattvas, and all the Buddha-
Tathagatas will always preach the Law to him. On
hearing it, he will keep the Law entirely and follow it
without disobeying. Moreover, he will interpret it
extensively for people as occasion calls. If the bodhisattva can hear one word or phrase of this sutra once,
twice, ten times, a hundred times, a thousand times,
myriad times, myriad kotis of times, or innumerable
and numberless times like the sands of the Ganges, he
will come to shake the three-thousand-great-thousand-
fold-world, though he cannot yet realize the ultimate
truth, and will take all great bodhisattvas into his
attendance, while being admired by all the four classes

and eight guardians, though he cannot yet roll the great Law wheel with the sacred voice like the roll of thunder. Entering deeply into the secret law of the Buddhas, he will interpret it without error or fault. He will always be protected by all the Buddhas, and especially covered with affection because he is a beginner in learning. This is called the fourth inconceivable merit-power of this sutra.

Good sons and daughters! Fifthly, the inconceivable merit-power of this sutra is as follows: If good sons or good daughters keep, read, recite and copy the Sutra of Innumerable Meanings, such a profound and supreme Great-vehicle, either during the Buddha's lifetime or after his extinction, they will realize the way of great bodhisattvas, though they cannot yet be delivered from all the faults of ordinary people and are still wrapped up in delusions. They will be filled with joy and convince those living beings, extending a day to a hundred kalpas, or shortening a hundred kalpas to a single day. These good sons and daughters are just like a dragon's son who can raise clouds and cause a rainfall seven days after his birth. This is the fifth inconceivable merit-power of this sutra.

Good sons and daughters! Sixthly, the inconceivable merit-power of this sutra is as follows: If any good sons or good daughters keep, read, recite and copy this sutra either during the Buddha's lifetime or after his extinction, even though clothed in delusions, they will deliver living beings from the life and death of delusions and make them overcome all sufferings by preaching the Law to them. After hearing it, living beings will put it into practice and attain the Law, the Merit and the Way. Suppose that a king, in journeying or falling ill, leaves the management of national affairs to his prince, though he still very young. Then the prince, by order of the great king, leads all the government officials according to the law, and propagates the right policies, so that every citizen of the country follows his orders exactly as if the king were governing. It is the same with good sons and good daughters who keep this sutra. During the Buddha's lifetime or after his extinction, these disciples will propagate the doctrine, preaching exactly as the Buddha did, though they themselves cannot yet live in the first steps of immobility, and if living beings, after hearing the preaching, practice it intently, they will cast off delusions and attain the Law, the Merit and the Way. This is called the sixth inconceivable merit-power of this sutra.

Good sons and daughters! Seventhly, the inconceivable merit-power of this sutra is as follows: If any good

sons or good daughters, upon hearing this sutra either
during the Buddha's lifetime or after his extinction,
rejoice, believe and raise the rare mind, keep, read,
recite, copy, practice it as it has been preached, aspire
to buddhahood, cause all the good roots to sprout, raise
the mind of great compassion, and desire to relieve all
living beings from suffering, the six Paramitas will be
naturally present in them, though they cannot yet
practice the six Paramitas. They will attain the assurance of the law of no birth in their bodies, life and
death and delusions will be instantly destroyed, and
they will raise to the seventh stage of bodhisattva.

Suppose there is a vigorous man who tries to destroy
an enemy on behalf of his king, and after the enemy
has been destroyed, with great joy, the king gives that
man half the kingdom as a reward. Good sons and
good daughters who keep this sutra are like this.
They are the most vigorous of all ascetics. They come
to attain the Law-treasure of the six Paramitas even
though they are not consciously seeking it. The enemy
of eternal life will be naturally destroyed, and these
good people will be comforted by the prize of a fief,
realizing the asurance of no birth in their bodies as the
treasure of half the buddha-country. This is called the
seventh inconceivable merit-power of this sutra.

The Sutra of Innumerable Meanings

Good sons and daughters! Eighthly, the inconceivable merit-power of this sutra is as follows: If good sons or good daughters, either during the Buddha's lifetime or after his extinction, see someone who has received this sutra, they will make him revere and believe it exactly as if he saw the body of the Buddha. They will keep, read, recite, copy and worship this sutra with joy, serve and practice it as the Law, firmly keep the commandments and persevere. They will also practice almsgiving, raise a deep benevolence, and explain the Sutra of Innumerable Meanings, such a supreme Great-vehicle, widely to others. To one who, for a long time does not recognize the existence of sinfulness and blessedness, they will show this sutra and it will force him to have faith with all sorts of expedients. By the strong power of this sutra, he will be made to stir up faith and to convert suddenly. After stirring up faith, he will endeavor so valorously that he will acquire the virtue and the power of this sutra, and attain the Merit and the Way. In this way, these good sons and good daughters will attain the assurance of the law of no birth in their bodies by the merit of having been enlightened, reach the upper stage of bodhisattva, become the attendants of the Buddhas, together with all the bodhisattvas convert living beings quickly, purify

The Sutra of Innumerable Meanings

Buddha lands, and attain supreme Buddhahood before long. This is called the eighth inconceivable merit-power of this sutra.

Good sons and daughters! Ninthly, the inconceivable merit-power of this sutra is as follows: If good sons or good daughters, upon receiving this sutra, either during the Buddha's lifetime or after his extinction, leap for joy, acquire the unprecedented, keep, read, recite, copy, adore and explain its meaning discriminately and widely for living beings, they will instantly destroy the heavy barrier of sins resulting from previous karmas and become purified, acquire great eloquence, gradually realize all paramitas, accomplish all samadhis and suramgama-samadhis, enter the great gate of dharani, and rise up to the upper stage of bodhisattva quickly. They will spread their divided bodies in all the lands of the ten directions, and relieve and emancipate entirely all living beings who suffer greatly in the twenty-four abodes. This is called the ninth inconceivable merit-power of this sutra.

Good sons and daughters! Tenthly, the inconceivable merit-power of this sutra is as follows: If good sons or good daughters, upon receiving this sutra either during the Buddha's lifetime or after his extinction, greatly rejoice, raise the rare mind for saving others, keep, read, recite, copy and adore this sutra of their own accord, practice it as it has been preached, and induce any monks or lay people to keep, read, recite, copy, adore and practice it as the Law, then these good sons and daughters will obtain the innumerable realms of dharani in their bodies because it is wholly by the merciful and friendly instructions of these good sons and good daughters that other people attain the Merit and the Way through the power of the practice of this sutra.

They will make countless vast oaths and great vows naturally and from the beginning in the days of ordinary people, and raise a deep desire to relieve all living beings from suffering. They will realize the great compassion, thoroughly abolish all sufferings, gather many good roots and bring benefit to all. They will explain the favor of the Law and greatly enliven the withered, give all living beings the medicine of the Law, set all at ease and gradually elevate their view to live in the stage of the Law-cloud. They will spread favor extensively, grant mercy to all suffering living beings, and lead them into the Way. Thereupon these disciples will accomplish Perfect Enlightenment before long. This is the tenth inconceivable merit-power of this sutra.

The Sutra of Innumerable Meanings

Good sons and daughters! The Sutra of Innumerable Meanings, such a supreme Great-vehicle, has an extremely great divine power and is unsurpassed in its worth. It makes all ordinary people accomplish the Sacred Merit, and makes them free from life and death forever. It makes all the living sprout the innumerable ways of all the bodhisattvas in the stage of ordinary people and makes the tree of merit grow dense, thick and tall. Therefore, this sutra is also called 'The Inconceivable Merit-Power Sutra.' "

At that time the Bodhisattva great Adornment rose up from his seat, went up to the Buddha and, along with the eighty thousand bodhisattvas, made obeisance at his feet, made processions around him, then going forth to kneel, said to the Buddha, "World-honored One! We have been placed under the mercy of the World-honored One to our delight. The Sutra of Innumerable Meanings, this profound, wonderful and supreme Great-vehicle has been preached for us. We will widely propagate this sutra after the Tathagata's extinction in obedience to the Buddha's command and let all keep, read, recite, copy and adore it. Be pleased to have no anxiety! With the vow-power, we will let all

137

the living observe, read, recite, copy and adore this sutra, and acquire the marvelous merits of this sutra."

At that time the Buddha said in praise, *"Excellent! Excellent! All good sons and daughters, you are persons who abolish sufferings and remove calamities thoroughly with great mercy and great compassion. You have been the great good leaders extensively for all. You are the great support for all living beings. You are the great benefactors of all living beings. Always bestow the benefits of the Law extensively for all."*

The Wonderful
Law-Flower Sutra

The Wonderful Law-Flower Sutra

Thus I have heard. After preaching the Sutra of Innumerable Meanings, the Buddha addressed the eighty thousand great bodhisattvas through the Bodhisattva Medicine King, saying, "*Medicine King! Do you see in this assembly innumerable heavenly beings, dragon kings, yakshas, gandharvas, asuras, garudas, kimnaras, mahorages, human and non-human beings, bhikshus, bhikshunis, male and female lay devotees, seekers after sravakaship, seekers after pratyekabuddhahood, seekers after bodhisattvaship and seekers after Buddhahood? All such beings as these, in the presence of the Buddha, if they hear a single verse or a single word of the Wonderful Law Flower Sutra and even by a single thought delight in it, I predict that they will attain Perfect Enlightenment.*

Moreover, after the extinction of the Tathagata, if there be any people who hear even a single verse or a single word of the Wonderful Law Flower Sutra and by a single thought delight in it, I also predict for them Perfect Enlightenment.

Again, let there be any who receive and keep, read and recite, copy and expound even a single verse of the Wonderful Law Flower Sutra and look upon this sutra with reverence as if it were the Buddha, and make offerings to it in various ways with flowers, perfumes, garlands, sandal powder, perfumed unguents, incense for burning, silk canopies, banners, flags, garments and music, as well as revere it with folded hands. Know, Medicine King! These people have already paid homage to ten myriad kotis of Buddhas and under the Buddhas performed their great vows. Therefore, out of compassion for all living beings, they are born here among ordinary people.

Medicine King! If there be any people who ask you what sort of living beings will become Buddhas in future worlds, you should show them that these are the people who will becomes Buddhas in future worlds. Wherefore? If any good sons or good daughters receive and keep, read and recite, expound and copy even a single word or verse of the Wonderful Law Flower Sutra and make offerings to it in various ways with flowers, perfumes, garlands, sandal powder, fragrant unguents, incense for burning, silk canopies, banners, flags, garments and music, as well as revere it with folded hands, these people will be looked up to by all the worlds, and as you pay homage to Tathagatas, so should you pay homage to them.

Know, Medicine King! These people are great bodhisattvas who, having accomplished Perfect Enlightenment and out of compassion for all living beings, are willingly born in this world and widely proclaim and expound the Wonderful Law Flower Sutra. How much more for those who are perfectly able to receive, keep and in every way pay homage to it!

Know, Medicine King! These people will of themselves abandon the recompense of their purified karmas and after my extinction, out of pity for all living beings, will be reborn in the Saha world and will widely proclaim this sutra. If these good sons and good daughters, after my extinction, should be able to preach to one person even one word or verse of the Wonderful Law Flower Sutra, know, these people are Tathagata-apostles sent by the Tathagata to perform Tathagata-deeds. How much more for those who, in great assemblies, widely preach it to others?

Medicine King! Even if there be some wicked person who out of an evil mind, throughout a whole kalpa, appears before the Buddha and unceasingly blasphemes the Buddha, his sin is still light, but if anyone, even with a single ill word, defames the lay devotees or bodhisattvas who read and recite the Wonderful Law Flower Sutra, his sin is extremely heavy.

Medicine King! He who reads and recites the Wonderful Law Flower Sutra, know! That one has adorned himself with the adornment of the Buddha, and so is carried by the Tathagata on his shoulder. Wherever he goes, he should be saluted with hands wholeheartedly folded, revered, worshipped, honored and extolled, and offerings made to him of flowers, perfumes, garlands, sandal powder, perfumed unguents, incense for burning, silk canopies, banners, flags, garments, edibles and dainties, and music. He should be served with the most excellent offerings found among people. He should be sprinkled with celestial jewels and offerings made of celestial jewels in heaps. Wherefore? It is because this person delights in preaching the Law. Those who hear it, but for a moment, thereupon attain Perfect Enlightenment.

Know, Medicine King! After the Tathagata is extinct those who are able to copy, keep, read, recite, worship and preach this sutra to others will be invested by the Tathagata with his robe and will be protected and remembered by Buddhas abiding in other regions. They shall have great powers of faith and the power of a resolute vow and the powers of virtuous character. Know, those people shall dwell with the Tathagata, and the Tathagata shall place his hand upon their heads.

Medicine King! Many people there are, both laymen and monks, who walk in the Bodhisattva Way, without, as it were, being able to see, hear, read, recite, copy, keep and worship the Wonderful Law Flower Sutra. Know that those people are not yet rightly walking in the Bodhisattva Way, but if any of them hear this sutra, then they will be able to walk aright in the Bodhisattva Way.

If any living beings who seek after the Bodhisattva Way either see or hear this Wonderful Law Flower Sutra, and after hearing or seeing it believe and discern, receive and keep it, you may know that they are near Perfect Enlightenment. Wherefore? It is because the Perfect Enlightenment of every bodhisattva all belongs to this sutra. This sutra brings out the fuller meaning of the tactful or partial method in order to reveal the real truth.

The treasury of this Wonderful Law Flower Sutra is so deep and so strong, so hidden and far away that no human being has been able to reach it. Now the Buddha has revealed it for instructing and perfecting bodhisattvas.

Medicine King! If any bodhisattva, upon hearing the Wonderful Law Flower Sutra is startled, doubts and fears, you may know that this is a bodhisattva neophyte. If any sravaka, upon hearing this sutra is startled, doubts and fears, you may know him for an arrogant person.

Medicine King! If there be any good son or good daughter who, after the extinction of the Tathagata, desires to preach this *Wonderful Law Flower Sutra* to the four groups, how should he preach it? That good son or good daughter, entering into the abode of the Tathagata, wearing the robe of the Tathagata, and sitting on the throne of the Tathagata, should then widely proclaim this sutra to the four groups of hearers. The abode of the Tathagata is the great compassionate heart within all living beings. The robe of the Tathagata is the gentle and forebearing heart. The throne of the Tathagata is the voidness of all existences.

Established in these, then with unflagging mind to the four groups of hearers he should preach this *Wonderful Law Flower Sutra.*

Medicine King! I, though dwelling in another realm, will send spirit messengers to gather together hearers of the Law for that preacher and also send spirit bhikshus, bhikshunis, and male and female lay devotees to hear his preaching of the Law. All these spirit people, upon hearing the Law, shall unresistingly receive it in faith and obey it.

If the preacher of the Law takes up his abode in a

secluded place, then I will abundantly send heavenly beings, dragons, spirits, gandharvas, asuras and others to hear him preach. Though I am in a different domain, I will from time to time cause the preacher of the Law to see me. If he forgets any detail of this sutra, I will return and tell it to him, so that he may be in perfect possession of it."

At that time the Bodhisattva Medicine King and the Bodhisattva Great Eloquence, along with the retinue of twenty thousand bodhisattvas, all in the presence of the Buddha, made this vow saying, "Be pleased, World-honored One, to be without anxiety! After the extinction of the Tathagata we will keep, read, recite and preach this sutra. In the evil age to come living beings will decrease in good qualities, while they will increase in utter arrogance and in covetousness of gain and honors, and will develop their evil qualities and be far removed from emancipation. Though it may be difficult to teach and convert them, we, arousing our utmost patience, will read and recite this sutra, keep, preach, copy, pay every kind of homage to it and spare not our body and life."

At that time the Bodhisattva Manjusri spoke

to the Buddha saying, "World-honored One! Rare indeed are such bodhisattvas as these! Reverently according with the Buddha, they have made great vows that in the evil age to come they will protect, keep, read, recite, copy and preach this Wonderful Law Flower Sutra. World-honored One! How will these bodhisattvas be able to preach this sutra in the evil age to come?"

The Buddha addressed Manjusri, saying, "*If any bodhisattva desires to preach this sutra in the evil age to come, he should be steadfast in the four methods. First, he should be steadfast in the bodhisattva's spheres of action and intimacy, so that he may be able to preach this sutra to living beings.*

Manjusri! Why is it called a bodhisattva's sphere of action? If a bodhisattva abides in a state of patience, is gentle and agreeable, is neither hasty nor overbearing and his mind is unperturbed, and if he has no delusions by which to act, but sees all things in their reality, nor does he proceed along the undivided way; this is called a bodhisattva's sphere of action.

Again, Manjusri! After the extinction of the Tathagata, in the period of the Decline of the Law, one who desires to preach this sutra should abide in the pleasant ministry of speech. Wherever he orally proclaims or reads this sutra, he takes no pleasure in telling of the errors of others, neither does he despise other preachers, nor does he speak of the good and evil, merits and demerits of other people, nor does he single out sravakas by name and publish their errors and sins, nor by name does he praise their excellences, nor does he beget an invidious mind. By keeping well such a cheerful heart as this, those who hear him will offer no opposition. To those who ask difficult questions, he does not answer with the law of the small vehicle but only with the law of the Great-vehicle and he explains it to them so that they may obtain perfect knowledge.

Again, Manjusri! The bodhisattva should, in the corrupt age to come when the Law is about to perish, receive and keep, read and recite, copy and adore this sutra, not cherish an envious and deceitful mind, nor slight and abuse other learners of the Buddha-Way and seek out their excesses and shortcomings. If there be any bhikshus, bhikshunis, male and female lay disciples who seek after sravakaship or seek after pratyekbuddhahood, or seek after the Bodhisattva Way, he does not distress them, causing them doubts and regrets by saying to them, 'You are far removed from the Way and will never be able to attain perfect knowledge. Why? It is because you are unstable people and remiss in the Way.'

Moreover, he should not indulge in discussions about the Law or engage in disputations, but in regard to all the living he should think of them with great compassion. In regard to the Tathagatas, he should think of them as benevolent fathers. In regard to the bodhisattvas, he should think of them as his great teachers. In regard to the universal great bodhisattvas, he should from the depth of his heart revere and worship them. In regard to all living beings, he should preach the Law equally, so as to accord with the Law, neither more nor less.

Manjusri! When this bodhisattva, in the last age, when the Law is about to perish, has accomplished this third pleasant ministry of thought and preaches this sutra nothing will be able to disturb him. He will find good companions who will read and recite this sutra with him. He will find a great multitude to come and hear him, who, after hearing are able to observe it, after observing are able to recite it, after reciting are able to preach it, after preaching are able to copy or cause others to copy it, and who will pay homage to the sutra, revering, honoring and extolling it.

Again, Manjusri! The bodhisattva, in the last age to come when the Law is about to perish, who keeps

The Wonderful Law-Flower Sutra

this *Wonderful Law Flower Sutra*, should beget a spirit
of great charity toward lay people and monks, and beget a spirit of great compassion for those who are not
yet bodhisattvas. And he should reflect thus, 'Such
people as these have suffered great loss. The Law
preached, as opportunity served, by the tactful method
of the Tathagata they have neither heard, nor known,
nor apprehended, nor inquired about, nor believed in
nor understood. Though these people have not inquired
about, nor believed in nor understood this sutra, when
I have attained Perfect Enlightenment, wherever I am,
by my transcendental powers and powers of wisdom, I
will lead them to abide in this Law.'

Manjusri! The bodhisattva, who, after the extinction of the Tathagata, has accomplished this fourth
pleasant ministry of thought, when he preaches the
Law will be free from errors. He will ever be worshiped,
revered, honored and extolled by bhikshus, bhikshunis,
male and female lay devotees, by kings and princes, by
ministers and Brahmanas, by citizens and others. All
the heavenly beings in the sky also, in order to hear the
Law, will always follow and attend on him. If he is in
a village or city or secluded forest and someone comes
desiring to put difficult questions to him, the heavenly
beings day and night, for the sake of the Law, will

151

constantly guard and protect him, so that he shall be able to cause all his hearers to rejoice. Wherefore? It is because this sutra is that which all past, future and present Buddhas watch over by their divine powers.

Manjusri! In countless countries even the name of this *Wonderful Law Flower Sutra* cannot be heard. How much less can it be seen, received and kept, read and recited? Manjusri! It is like a powerful holy wheel-rolling king who desires by force to conquer other domains. When minor kings do not obey his command, the wheel-rolling king calls up his various armies and goes to punish them. The king, seeing the soldiers who distinguish themselves in battle, is greatly pleased and, according to their merit, bestows rewards either giving them fields, houses, villages or cities, or giving garments or personal ornaments, or giving all kinds of treasures, gold, silver, lapis lazuli, moonstones, agates, coral, amber, elephants, horses, carriages and litters. Only the crown jewel worn on his head he gives to no one. Wherefore? It is because only on the head of a king may this sole jewel be worn, and if he gives it away, all the king's retinue would be astounded.

Manjusri! The Tathagata is also like this. By his powers of meditation and wisdom he has taken possession of the domain of the Law and rules as king over the triple world. But the Mara kings are unwilling to submit. The Tathagata's wise and holy generals fight with them. With those who distinguish themselves he, too, is pleased, and in the midst of his four hosts preaches this Wonderful Law Flower Sutra to them, causing them to rejoice and bestows on them the meditations, the emancipations, the faultless roots and powers, and all the wealth of the Law. In addition, he gives them the city of Nirvana, saying that they have attained extinction, and attracts their minds so that they will rejoice. Yet, he does not preach to them the Wonderful Law Flower Sutra.

Manjusri! Just as the powerful wheel-rolling king, seeing his soldiers who distinguish themselves, is so extremely pleased that now, at last, he gives them the incredible jewel so long worn on his head, which may not wantonly be given to anyone, so also is it with the Tathagata.

As the great Law-king of the triple world, teaching and converting all the living by the Law, when he sees his wise and holy army fighting with the Mara of the mental processes, the Mara of earthly cares, the Mara of desires and the Mara of death, and doing so with great exploits and merits, exterminating the three poisons of greed, anger and delusion, escaping from the

*triple world and breaking through the nets of Mara,
then the Tathagata also is greatly pleased, and now,
at last, preaches this Wonderful Law Flower Sutra
which has never before been preached, and which is
able to cause all the living to reach perfect knowledge,
though all the world greatly resents and has difficulty
in believing it.*

*Manjusri! This Wonderful Law Flower Sutra is the
foremost teaching of the Tathagatas and the most profound of all discourses. I give it to you last of all, just
as the powerful wheel-rolling king at last gives the
brilliant jewel he has guarded for so long.*

*Manjusri! This Wonderful Law Flower Sutra is the
mysterious treasury of the Buddha-Tathagatas, which
is supreme above all sutras. For a long time it has been
guarded and not prematurely declared. Today, for the
first time, I proclaim it to you all!"*

Then the Buddha addressed the bodhisattvas
and the great assembly, *"Believe and discern, all you
good sons and daughters, the Tathagata's word of
Truth. Listen each of you to the secret, mysterious and
supernatural power of the Tathagata.*

*All the worlds of heavenly beings, men and asuras
declare: 'Now has Sakyamuni-Buddha, coming forth
from the palace of the Sakya-clan, and seated at the*

place of enlightenment, not far from the city of Gaya, attained to Perfect Enlightenment.'

Good sons and daughters! Since I veritably became Buddha, there have passed infinite, boundless, thousands, myriads of kotis of kalpas. For instance, suppose there were five hundred thousand myriad kotis of numberless three-thousand-great-thousandfold-worlds. Let someone grind them to powder and pass eastward through five hundred thousand myriad numberless countries, and then drop one of these particles, proceeding eastward until he finishes dropping every one of these particles. What do you think? Is it possible to imagine and calculate all those worlds so as to know their number?

Good sons and daughters! Now I must clearly announce and declare it to you. Suppose you take in powder form all of these worlds, everywhere that a particle has been deposited, and everywhere that it has not been deposited, and count a particle as a kalpa. The time since I became the Buddha still surpasses these by hundreds, thousands, myriads of kotis of numberless kalpas. From that time forward I have constantly been preaching and teaching in this Saha-world, and also leading and benefitting the living in other places in hundreds, thousands, myriads of kotis of numberless domains. During this time, I have spoken of the Buddha 'Burning Light' and other Buddhas, and also have told of their entering Nirvana. Thus have I tactfully described them all. Whenever living beings came to me, I beheld with a Buddha's Eye all their faculties, whether keen or dull, and also their level of faith, and so on. And I explained to them, in stage after stage, according to their capacity and their degree of understanding, my different names and the length of my lives, and moreover plainly stated that I must enter Nirvana. I also, with various expedients, preached the Wonderful Law Flower Sutra, which is able to cause the living to beget a joyful heart.

Good sons and daughters! All the sutras, which the Tathagata preaches, are for the deliverance of the living. They are real, and not empty air. Wherefore? It is because the Tathagata knows and sees the character of the triple world as it really is. To him there is neither birth nor death, neither going away nor coming, neither existence in the world nor cessation of existence, neither reality nor unreality, neither thus nor otherwise. Unlike the way the triple world sees itself, the Tathagata sees the triple world clearly, without mistake. Because all the living have various natures, various desires, various activities, various ideas and reasonings, so, the Tatha-

gata by so many reasonings preaches the Truth, causing the living to sprout the roots of goodness.

Thus it is, since I became Buddha in the far distant past, that my lifetime is of numberless kalpas, forever existing and immortal.

Good sons and daughters! The lifetime that I fulfill in following the Bodhisattva Way is not even yet completed, but will be again twice the previous number of kalpas. Now in this unreal Nirvana, I announce that I must enter the real Nirvana. In this expedient way the Tathagata teaches all the living. Wherefore? If the Buddha abides long in the world, then people of little virtue; those who do not cultivate the roots of goodness and are spiritually poor and mean, greedily attached to the five desires, and caught in the net of wrong reflection and false views; such people as these, if they see the Tathagata constantly present and not extinct, will become puffed up and lazy, and unable to conceive of the idea that it is difficult to meet a Buddha, and will be unable to develop a mind of reverence for him.

Therefore the Tathagata tactfully says, 'Know, Bodhisattvas! The appearance of a Buddha in the world is a rare occurrence.' Wherefore? In the course of countless hundreds of thousands of myriads of kotis of kalpas, some people of little virtue may happen to see a Buddha, or none may see him. For this reason I say, 'Bodhisattvas! A Tathagata may rarely be seen!'

All living beings, upon hearing such a statement, must indeed realize the thought of the difficulty of meeting a Buddha and cherish a longing and a thirst for him. Thus will they cultivate the roots of goodness. Therefore the Tathagata, though he does not in reality become extinct, yet announces his extinction.

Good sons and daughters! If there be any who have faith in the Eternal Life of the Buddha, he will see the Buddha always on the Spiritual Vulture Peak surrounded by his celestial host ever preaching the Law.

Goods sons and daughters! If anyone, after my extinction, hears this Sutra, and is able to receive and keep it, copy or cause others to copy it, then he has already erected monasteries and built red sandalwood temples of thirty-two shrines, tall as eight Tala-trees, lofty, spacious, splendid, in which abide hundreds of thousands of bhikshus adorned also with gardens, promenades, groves and bathing pools. Such monasteries and such numbers of temples as these he has, here in my presence, offered to me and my bhikshu-monks.

Therefore I say, if anyone after the extinction of

*the Tathagata, receives and keeps, reads and recites,
copies or causes others to copy, and pays homage to
this Sutra, he need no longer erect stupas and temples,
or build monasteries and make offerings to the monks.
How much more for the ones who are able to keep this
Sutra and add almsgiving, morality, forbearance, zeal,
concentration and wisdom? His merit will be most
excellent, infinite and boundless. Even as the sky which
is east, west, south and north, the four intermediate
directions, the zenith and nadir, is infinite and boundless, so also the merits of this person will be infinite
and boundless, and he will speedily reach Perfect
Knowledge.*

*If anyone hears this Wonderful Law Flower Sutra,
even momentarily, his merit is so great that in his next
rebirth he will acquire the most excellent kinds of elephants, horses, jewelled palanquins and litters, and
ride in celestial carriages.*

*If the merits of a hearer of this sutra are so vast, how
much greater for those who, in great assemblies, preach
it?"*

At that time the Bodhisattva Universal Virtue, with sovereign supernatural power, majesty
and fame, accompanied by great bodhisattvas,
unlimited, infinite and incalculable, came from

159

the eastern quarter. The countries through which
he passed were shaken, jeweled lotus flowers
rained down and countless hundred thousand
myriad kotis of kinds of music were performed.
Encompassed also by a great host of countless
heavenly beings, dragons, yakshas, gandharvas,
asuras, garudas, kimnaras, mahorages, human
and non-human beings, all displaying majestic
supernatural powers, he arrived at Mount Grdhrakuta in the Saha world. Having prostrated
himself before Sakyamuni Buddha, he made
processions around him to the right seven times
and addressed the Buddha, saying, "World-
honored One! I, in the domain of the Buddha
Jeweled Majestic Superior King, hearing afar
that the Wonderful Law Flower Sutra was being
preached in this Saha world, have come with this
host of countless, infinite hundred thousand
myriad kotis of bodhisattvas to hear and receive
it. Be pleased, World-honored One, to tell us
how good sons and good daughters will be able
to obtain this Wonderful Law Flower Sutra after
the extinction of the Tathagata."

The Buddha replied to the Bodhisattva
Universal Virtue, "*If any good son or good daughter*

acquires the four requisites, such a one as this will obtain this Wonderful Law Flower Sutra after the extinction of the Tathagata. First, one is to be under the guardianship of the Buddhas. Second, one is to plant the roots of virtue. Third, one is to enter the assembly of people of correct resolution. Fourth, one is to aspire after the salvation of all the living. Any good son or good daughter who acquires these four requisites will certainly obtain this sutra after the extinction of the Tathagata."

At that time the Bodhisattva Universal Virtue said to the Buddha, "World-honored One! In the latter five hundred years of the corrupt and evil age, whoever receives and keeps this sutra, I will guard and protect, eliminate the anxiety of falling away and give ease of mind, so that no spy shall find occasion; neither Mara, nor Mara-sons, nor Mara-daughters, nor Mara-people, nor yakshas, nor rakshasas, nor putanas, nor vetadas, nor other afflicters of people; that none may find an occasion to harm the bearer of this sutra.

Wherever such a person walks or stands, reading and reciting this sutra, I will at once mount the six-tusked white elephant king and, along with a host of great bodhisattvas, go to that place and, showing myself to him, will serve and protect him, comforting his mind, thereby serving this sutra.

Wherever such a person sits, pondering this sutra, I will again mount the six-tusked white elephant king and show myself to him. If such a one forgets, be it but a single word or verse of the Wonderful Law Flower Sutra, I will teach it to him, read and recite it with him, and again cause him to master it. Thereupon anyone who receives and keeps, reads and recites the Wonderful Law Flower Sutra upon seeing me will greatly rejoice and renew his zeal.

Through seeing me he will thereupon acquire the contemplations and dharanis named the dharani of revolution, the dharani of hundreds of thousands of revolutions, and the dharani of skill in Law-sounds. Such dharanis as these will he acquire.

World-honored One! If, in the last five hundred years of the corrupt and evil age, the bhikshus, bhikshunis, upasakas, seekers, receivers and keepers, readers, reciters and copiers of the Wonderful Law Flower Sutra desire to put into practice this sutra, they must single mindedly devote themselves to it for three times seven days. After the three times seven days are fulfilled, I will again mount the six-tusked white elephant king and, together with countless bodhisattvas surrounding me, appear before these people in the form that all the living delight to see and preach to them, revealing, instructing, benefitting and rejoicing them.

Moreover, I will give them dharanis and upon obtaining these dharanis, no human or non-human being can harm them. I myself also will ever protect them. If, while the Wonderful Law Flower Sutra proceeds on its course through Jambudvipa, there be any who receive and keep it, let them reflect thus, 'This is all due to the majestic power of Universal Virtue.'

If any receive and keep, read and recite, rightly remember and practice it as preached, let it be known that these people are doing the works of Universal Virtue and have deeply planted good roots under numerous countless Buddhas, and that their heads will be caressed by the hands of the Tathagatas.

If they only copy this sutra, then these when their lives are ended will be born into the Trayastrimsa Heaven, on which occasion eighty-four thousand heavenly nymphs, performing all kinds of celestial music will come to welcome them, and they, wearing seven-jeweled crowns, will joy and delight among those beautiful nymphs. How much more for those who receive and keep, read and recite, rightly remember and practice it as preached!

If there be any who receive and keep, read and recite this sutra, when their life is ended the hands of a thousand Buddhas will be proffered, so that they do not fear, neither will they fall into any evil destiny, but instead they will go straight to Maitreya Buddha in the Tusita Heaven, where Maitreya Buddha, possessed of the thirty-two signs, is surrounded by a host of great bodhi-sattvas and hundreds of thousands of myriads of kotis of heavenly nymph followers, amongst whom they will be born. Such are their merits and rewards.

Therefore, the wise should with all their might themselves copy this sutra or cause others to copy it, receive and keep, read and recite, rightly remember and practice it as preached.

World-honored One! I now by my supurnatural power will guard and protect this sutra so that, after the extinction of the Tathagata, it may spread abroad without cease in Jambudvipa."

Sakyamuni Buddha extolled him, saying, "It is well, it is well, Universal Virtue, that you are able to protect and assist this sutra, and bring happiness and weal to the living in many places. You have already attained inconceivable merits and profound benevolence and compassion. From a long distant past you have aspired to Perfect Enlightenment and been able to make this supernatural vow to guard and protect this sutra. And I, by my supernatural power, will guard and protect those who are able to receive and keep the name of the Bodhisattva Universal Virtue.

Universal Virtue! If there be any who receive and keep, read and recite, rightly remember, practice and copy this Wonderful Law Flower Sutra, know that such people as these are attending on Sakyamuni Buddha as if they were hearing this sutra from the Buddha's mouth. Know that such people are paying homage to Sakyamuni Buddha. Know that the Buddha is praising them, 'Well done.'

Know that the heads of these people are being caressed by the hands of Sakyamuni Buddha. Know that these people are covered by the robe of Sakyamuni

The Wonderful Law-Flower Sutra

Buddha.

These people will not again be eager for worldly pleasures, nor will they be fond of heretical scriptures and writings, nor will they ever again take pleasure in intimacy with evil people. But persons such as these will be right-minded, have high moral character and be auspicious.

They will not be harassed by the three poisons - anger, greed and delusion - nor will they be harassed by envy, pride, haughtiness and arrogance. These people will be content with few desires and able to do the works of Universal Virtue.

Universal Virtue! After the extinction of the Tath-agata, in the latter five hundred years of the corrupt and evil age, if anyone sees someone who receives and keeps, reads and recites, the Wonderful Law Flower Sutra, he must reflect thus, 'This person will before long go to the wisdom floor, destroy the host of Mara, attain Perfect Enlightenment and rolling onward the Law-wheel, beating the Law-drum, blowing the Law-conch, and pouring the rain of the Law, shall sit on the lion throne of the Law amidst a great assembly of heavenly beings and people.'

Universal Virtue! Whoever in future ages shall receive and keep, read and recite this sutra, such persons as these will no longer be greedily attached to clothes, bed things, drink, food and things for the support of life. Whatever they wish will never be in vain, and in this present life they will obtain their blessed reward. If anyone takes offerings to and praises them, he will obtain visible reward in this present life.

Therefore, Universal Virtue, if anyone sees someone who has received and kept this sutra, he should stand up and greet them from afar, just as if he were paying reverence to the Buddha."

While this chapter of the encouragement of the Bodhisattva Universal Virtue was being preached, innumerable incalculable bodhisattvas equal to the sands of the Ganges attained the dharanis of the hundreds of thousands of myriads of kotis of revolutions, and bodhisattvas became perfect in the way of Universal Virtue.

After the Buddha preached this sutra, Universal Virtue and the other bodhisattvas, Sariputra and the other sravakas, and the heavenly beings, dragons, human and non-human beings, and all others in the great assembly greatly rejoiced together and, taking possession of the sutra, made salutation to the Buddha and withdrew.

*Prophecies Concerning
the Future Buddha, Maitreya*

Prophecies Concerning the Future Buddha, Maitreya

Thus I have heard. On a certain occasion the Buddha was staying at Kapilavatthu in Banyon Grove on the banks of the Rohani River. At that time the venerable Sariputra questioned the Blessed One concerning the future Buddha,
"The Hero that shall follow you,
As Buddha, what sort is he?
The account in full I wish to learn,
Tell it to me, All Seeing One."
Then the Buddha replied to Sariputra,
"I'll tell it to you Sariputra,
Pray lend your ears, for I will speak.
Our cycle is a happy one,
Three Buddhas have already lived; Kakusandha,
Konagamana, and the leader Kassapa.
The Buddha now supreme am I,
But after me Maitreya comes
In the latter years of this same auspicious age.
By name, supreme of all men,
The perfect Buddha Maitreya,
Will be known as the Friendly One,
Who shall widely save living creatures,
Countless in number.

Prophecies Concerning the Future Buddha, Maitreya

*Bhikshus, just as I am Araham, being worthy of
special veneration, Sammasan-buddha, having truly
comprehended all the dhammas by my own intellect
and insight, being endowed with supreme knowledge
and perfect practice of morality, speaking only words
that are true and beneficial, knowing all the three
lokas and being incomparable in taming those who
deserve to be tamed, Buddha, being the Enlightened
One and Bhagava, being the Most Exalted One, have
at this time appeared in this world, so also there will
appear in this world a Buddha called Maitreya.*

*This Buddha will also be a Bhagava who is Ara-
ham, being worthy of special veneration, Samma-sam-
buddha, having truly comprehended all the dhammas
with his own intellect and insight, being endowed with
supreme knowledge and perfect practice of morality,
speaking only words that are true and beneficial, knowing all the three lokas and being incomparable in taming those who deserve to be tamed, Buddha, being the
Enlightened One.*

*Just as I now teach the Dharma, which is good in
the beginning, good in the middle and good in the end,
rich in meaning and words, and just as I make clear
the completeness and purity of the Noble Practice, so
also the Maitreya Buddha will teach the Dharma. His*

Prophecies Concerning the Future Buddha, Maitreya

Dharma will also be good in the beginning, good in the middle and good in the end, rich in meanings and words, and will make clear the completeness and purity of the Noble Practice.

Just as I am perfected in the ten virtues, so also the Maitreya Buddha will be perfected in the ten virtues. He will be especially perfected in the virtue of Dana, by donating his own life in order to save others.

Just as I am accompanied by hundreds of followers when traveling, the Maitreya Buddha will be accompanied by thousands of followers when traveling.

The Perfectly Self-Enlightened Maitreya Buddha will go forth from the household life to the homeless life of an ascetic. After thus renouncing the world, he will live alone and in seclusion, vigilant and zealous, will incline his mind toward Nirvana and will soon attain, by himself, in this very life by virtue of Magga Knowledge, the fruits of the noblest and most supreme Arahatship, the ultimate goal for which men of good families forsake hearth and home to lead the homeless life.

Who will not see Maitreya, the Blessed One, and who will see him?

Those who are born into the Avici hells for performing the five crimes that constitute 'proximate karma' –

the killing of one's own mother, the killing of one's own father, the killing of a monk, the killing of a nun, the cherishing of heretical views - will not see him.

Those who slander the noble disciples will not see him.

The naked ascetics who create a schism by denying the congregation allowable privileges will not see him.

All other beings who give gifts, keep the precepts, keep fast days, fulfill their religious duties, found shrines, plant sacred fig trees, parks and groves, make bridges, clear the highways and dig wells will see him.

Those who, in their longing for a Blessed One, shall make a gift even if only a handful of flowers, or a single lamp or a mouthful of food will see him.

Those who feel pleasure at performing meritorious deeds will see him.

Those who further the religion of the Buddha, prepare the pavilion and seat the preachers of the Law, bring forward the fan, make offerings of cloth, canopies, garlands, incense or lamps will see him.

Those who give to the congregation offerings of food and clothes will see him.

Those who wait on their mothers and fathers and perform respectful duties for their elders among their kinsfolk will see him.

Prophecies Concerning the Future Buddha, Maitreya

*Those who practice the ten means of acquiring
merit will see him.*

*Maitreya Buddha will assist those who have gained
merit during the lifetime of Gotama Buddha to ferry
safely across the ocean of samsara to attain Nirvana.
That ocean of samsara is fed by the river waters of
desire, and is filled with the water of suffering with
its waves of birth, old age, sickness and death.*

*Maitreya Buddha saves those who are sunk in the
ocean of samsara and are about to fall into the furnace
of hell.*

*While the Maitreya Buddha saves the world by
preahing his dharma, his followers enter the sangha
with Maitreya's simple inducement, 'Come, disciple!'*

*The sangha of Maitreya will be known throughout
the whole world. All of Jambudvipa will be illuminated
by the light of robes worn by the disciples of his order.
By the touch or breeze against Maitreya's robes or body
while visiting the houses of lay devotees, all sorts of
diseases will disappear. On occasion Maitreya will
travel through the towns, villages and cities of Jambudvipa accompanied by his great disciples in order
to teach the people. His disciples, when they have
understood the doctrine of the blessed Maitreya
Buddha, will be known as Saints."*

The Gospel of Jesus the Christ
(Circa 5 B.C. – 28 A.D.)

The Gospel of Jesus the Christ

Circumstances Surrounding The Birth Of Jesus

There was in the days of Herod, the king of Judea, a certain priest named Zachariah who had a wife named Elizabeth. They were both pure and righteous before God, observing all of the commandments of the Lord blameless. They didn't have any children because Elizabeth was barren, and they both were now well into old age.

And it came to pass, that while Zachariah was executing his duties of the burning of the incense at the temple, an angel appeared in front of him standing on the right side of the altar of incense. When Zachariah saw him, he became troubled and was very afraid. The angel said to him, "Do not be afraid, your prayer has been answered. Your wife, Elizabeth, will bear a son and you will call his name John. You will have joy and gladness and many people will rejoice at his birth because he shall be great in the sight of the Lord. He will not drink wine or any strong drink and he will be filled with the Holy Spirit, even from his mother's womb. He will cause many of the children of Israel to turn to the Lord their God. He will go forward in the spirit and power of

Elijah to turn the hearts of the fathers to the children, the disobedient to the wisdom of the just and make the people prepared for the Lord." Zachariah said to the angel, "How can I believe this? I am an old man, and my wife is also very old." The angel replied, "I am Gabriel who stands in the presence of God, and I am sent to speak with you and to show you this good news. Behold! You shall be struck dumb and not able to speak until the day that these things come to pass because you do not believe my words, which will be fulfilled in their season."

The people waiting outside for Zachariah to complete his priestly duties began to wonder why he stayed so long in the temple. When Zachariah finally came out, he could not speak to them. They thought that he had seen a vision in the temple because he made signs to them, but he remained speechless. After completing his duties, Zachariah returned to his own house. Soon afterward his wife Elizabeth conceived, and she hid herself for five months saying, "This is how the Lord has dealt with me to take away my disgrace among men."

In the sixth month of Elizabeth's pregnancy

the angel, Gabriel, was sent from God to a city in Galilee called Nazareth. He was sent to a virgin named Mary who was engaged to a man named Joseph, who was of the house of David. The angel came to her and said, "Behold, you are very fortunate because the Lord is with you! Blessed are you among women!" When Mary heard this she became troubled and wondered about this manner of greeting. The angel said, "Don't be afraid, Mary, because you have found favor with God. And behold! You will conceive and bring forth a son, and you shall call his name Jesus. He shall be great and shall be called the Son of the Highest, and God shall give him the throne of his father, David. He shall reign over the house of Jacob forever, and there will be no end to his kingdom." Then Mary said to the angel, "How can this be, since I have never known a man?" The angel answered, "The Holy Spirit will come upon you and the power of the Highest will over-shadow you. Therefore this Holy Being, which will be born of you, shall be called the Son of God. And behold! Your cousin Elizabeth has also conceived a son in her old age. This is the sixth month with her who was called barren, for with

God nothing is impossible." Mary said, "Behold, the handmaid of the Lord, be it done unto me according to your word!" And the angel departed from her.

Afterward, Mary got up and went into the hill country, to a city in Judah and entered into the house of Zachariah where she greeted Elizabeth. As soon as Elizabeth heard Mary's greeting, the baby leapt inside her womb and Elizabeth was filled with the Holy Spirit. She spoke in a loud voice saying, "Blessed are you among women, and blessed is the fruit of your womb! What does this mean that the mother of my Lord should come to me? As soon as I heard your greeting, the baby leaped for joy in my womb." Mary said, "My soul praises the Lord, and my spirit has rejoiced in God my Savior. He has regarded the low state of His handmaiden because from now on all generations shall call me blessed. For He that is mighty has done great things to me, and Holy is His name." Mary stayed with Elizabeth about three months, and then she returned to her own house.

Now, Elizabeth's full time came and she delivered a son. Her neighbors and her cousins heard how God had showed great mercy on her, and they rejoiced with her. And it came to pass, that on the eighth day they came to circumcise the child and they called him Zachariah, after his father. Elizabeth said, "Not so, he shall be called John." They said to her, "There is no one in your family or kinsfolk that is called by this name." They made signs to his father asking him how he wanted the baby to be named. He motioned for a writing tablet and he wrote, "His name is John." And immediately his mouth was opened and his tongue loosed, and he spoke and praised God. All of the people there were astounded, and they went and reported what they had seen and heard throughout all of the hill country of Judea. And everyone who heard them would say, "What kind of child will this be?"

Zachariah was filled with the Holy Spirit and prophesied saying, "Blessed be the Lord God of Israel, because he has visited and redeemed his people and has sounded the trumpet of salvation for us in the house of his servant David. Just as he spoke by the mouth of his holy prophets that we shall be saved from our enemies and from all who hate us, he performs the mercy promised to our fathers and remembers his holy covenant that is the oath he made to our father Abraham. And you, my child, will be called the prophet of the Highest, because you will go ahead of the Lord and prepare his way. To give knowledge of salvation to his people by the remission of their sins, to give light to those that sit in darkness and in the shadow of death, and to guide our feet to walk in peace." The child grew and waxed strong in Spirit, and he stayed in the deserts until the day he showed himself to Israel.

Now when Jesus' mother, Mary, was found to be with child, Joseph, being a kind man and not wanting to expose her publicly was planning to break the engagement quietly. While he thought on these things an angel sent from God appeared to Joseph in a dream, saying, "Joseph, son of David, do not be afraid to take Mary to be your wife. The child, who is conceived in her, is of the Holy Spirit. She will bear a son and you will call him Jesus, and he will save his people from their sins." All of this came to pass so that it would be fulfilled that which was spoken by the prophet, "Behold, a virgin shall be with child and shall bring forth a son whose name being interpreted is 'God with us.' "

Joseph woke and did as the angel had commanded and took Mary to be his wife, but they did not know each other as husband and wife until she bore her firstborn son.

The Birth Of Jesus The Christ

In those days Caesar Augustus ordered a census for everyone to be counted and taxed in his or her own cities. Joseph went up from Galilee to Judea to the city called Bethlehem, since he was of the house and lineage of David. His wife Mary, being pregnant with Jesus, went with him into the city of Bethlehem. While they were there she began to deliver the baby. She delivered her firstborn son and wrapped him in strips of cloth and laid him in a manger, because there was no room for them at the inn.

In that same country there were shepherds staying in the field, keeping watch over their flock. An angel of the Lord came upon them, and the glory of the Lord shone round about them and they became very afraid. The angel said to them, "Do not be afraid. Behold, I bring you good tidings of great joy, which shall extend to all nations. For unto you is born this day in the city of David a Savior. This shall be a sign given to you: You will find the babe wrapped in swaddling clothes, lying in a manger." Suddenly there was with the angel a multitude of the heavenly host praising God and saying, "Glory to God in the highest, peace on earth, and good will toward men."

When the angels had gone away from them into heaven, the shepherds said to each other, "Let us go to Bethlehem and see this thing which has come to pass, which God has made known to us." They came with haste and found Mary and Joseph, and the babe lying in a manger. After they had seen, they reported abroad the sayings that were told to them concerning this child. Everyone who heard these things wondered at what was told to them by the shepherds. And the shepherds returned, glorifying and praising God because of what they had heard and seen.

After eight days, the baby was brought for the circumcision of the child and his name was called Jesus, which was so named by the angel before he was conceived in the womb.

The Gospel of Jesus the Christ

The Magi Come To Visit Jesus

Now, when Jesus was born in Bethlehem during the reign of King Herod, wise men from the east came to Jerusalem saying, "Where is He that is born King of the Jews? We have seen his star in the east and have come to worship him." When Herod, the king, heard this he became very troubled. Herod gathered all the chief priests and scribes together and demanded them to tell him where the Messiah was to be born. They said to him, "In Bethlehem of Judea because it was written by the prophets, 'And you, Bethlehem in the land of Judah, are not the least among the princes of Judah. Out of you shall come a Governor that shall rule my people Israel.' "

Then Herod brought the three wise men to him secretly and asked them when the star first appeared. Herod sent the Magi to Bethlehem saying, "Go and search for the young child, and when you have found him bring word to me, so that I may come and worship him also."

The Magi departed and the star, which they saw in the east, went ahead of them until it stood over the house where Jesus, Mary and Joseph were staying. When they came to this place they saw Jesus with Mary his mother, and they fell down and worshiped him. They presented Jesus with gifts of gold, frankincense and myrrh.

After being warned by God in a dream that they should not return to Herod, the Magi left for their own country taking another route back. After the three wise men left, an angel appeared to Joseph in a dream saying, "Get up, take the young child and his mother, and flee into Egypt. Stay there until I contact you. Herod will look for the child in order to destroy him." Joseph awoke and took Jesus and his mother, Mary, into Egypt.

As soon as Herod realized that he had been fooled by the wise men, he became very angry. Herod ordered all of the children in Bethlehem and in all the coastal areas that were two years old and younger to be killed. Then was fulfilled that which was spoken by the prophet Jeremy, "In Rama there was a voice heard, lamentation, weeping and great mourning; Rachael crying for her children and she could not be comforted, because they are no more."

After Herod died, an angel appeared to Joseph in a dream saying, "Get up, take the young child and his mother, and go into the land of Israel. Those who sought to destroy the child are now dead." Joseph got up, took Jesus and Mary, and they went into the land of Israel. Thus the prophecy was fulfilled, "Out of Egypt I have called my Son."

When Joseph heard that Archelaus, the son of Herod, reigned in Judea he was afraid to go there. After being warned by God in a dream, Joseph went into Galilee instead, into the city of Nazareth. So the prophecy was fulfilled, "He shall be called a Nazarene." The child grew and waxed strong in Spirit, filled with wisdom, and the grace of God was upon him.

Jesus Teaches In The Temple As A Child

Now, Jesus' parents went to Jerusalem every year at the feast of the Passover. And when he was twelve years old, they went up to Jerusalem after the custom of the feast. When they had fulfilled these days, as they returned, the child Jesus stayed behind in Jerusalem without the knowledge of Mary and Joseph. And they, assuming that Jesus was with the group, traveled a day's journey before realizing that he was missing. When they couldn't find him, they turned back to Jerusalem to look for him.

After three days they found him sitting in the temple, listening to the priests and asking them questions. Everyone there who heard him was astonished at his understanding and answers.

When Mary and Joseph saw him they were amazed and Mary said to him, "Son, your father and I have been looking for you! Why have you caused us such grief?" Jesus said to them, *"Why were you looking for me? Don't you know that I must be about my Father's business?"*

They didn't understand what he meant by this, and he left with them and was subjected under them, but his mother remembered his sayings in her heart. And Jesus increased in wisdom and stature, and in favor with God and man.

The Gospel of Jesus the Christ

John The Baptist Prepares The Way For Jesus

It was written by the prophets, "Behold, I
send a messenger who will prepare the way for
the Lord. To the voice of one crying in the
wilderness: Prepare the way for the Lord, make
his path straight."

John did baptize in the wilderness and preach
the baptism of repentance for the remission of
sins. People went out to him from Jerusalem,
Judea and the entire region around Jordan.
They were baptized by him in the river of Jordan,
confessing their sins. John wore clothes made
from camels' hair and a girdle of skin around his
loins, and he ate locusts and wild honey. He
preached saying, "There comes One mightier
than I after me, the latchets of whose shoes I am
not worthy to stoop down and unloose. I indeed
have baptized you with water, but he will baptize
you with the Holy Spirit."

Jesus came from Nazareth of Galilee and was
baptized by John in the river of Jordan. When
Jesus was baptized he went straightway out of the
water and the heavens were opened up to him,
and the Spirit of God descended upon him like

a dove. A voice from heaven said, "This is my beloved Son, in whom I am well pleased."
The Spirit immediately drove Jesus into the wilderness.

The Temptation Of Jesus

After he had fasted forty days and forty nights, Jesus became very hungry. Then Satan came to him and said, "If you really are the Son of God, then command these stones to be made into bread." Jesus said to him, *It is written: 'Man shall not live by bread alone, but by every word that proceeds out of the mouth of God.'* "
Then the Devil took him up to the holy city and sat him on top of the temple. Satan said to him, "If you really are the Son of God, then throw yourself down, for it is written: 'He will give his angels charge concerning him, and in their hands they will lift him up, so that he will not strike his foot against a stone.' "
Jesus said to him, *"It is also written: 'Do not put the Lord your God to the test.'* "
Then the Devil took Jesus up to a very high mountaintop and showed him all the kingdoms

of the world along with all their riches and said, "All of these things I will give to you if you will bow down and worship me."

Jesus said to him, *"Get away from me Satan! It is written: 'Worship only the Lord your God and serve him only.' "*

Then the devil left Jesus and the angels came and ministered to him.

Jesus Begins To Teach The Doctrine

After Jesus heard that John the Baptist had been thrown into prison, he went into Galilee. From that time on Jesus began to preach, *"Repent, for the kingdom of heaven is near."*

As Jesus was walking by the Sea of Galilee he saw two brothers, Simon called Peter, and his brother Andrew. They were casting their nets into the sea, for they were fishermen. Jesus said to them, *"Come and follow me, and I will make you fishers of men."* Right away they left their nets and followed Jesus.

Going on from there, Jesus saw two other brothers, James the son of Zebedee and his brother John. They were in a boat with their father, mending their nets. Jesus called out to them and they immediately left the boat and their father and followed him. Jesus went out around all of Galilee, teaching in the synagogues and healing all manner of sickness and disease among the people. His fame spread throughout all of Syria.

People brought to him all kinds of sick people that were tormented and had various diseases. There were those who were possessed with demons, and insane people, and those who had the palsy. Jesus healed them all.

Great multitudes of people followed him from Galilee and from Decapolis, and from Jerusalem and from beyond Jordan. Upon seeing the multitudes, Jesus went up to the top of a mountain and sat down. Then his disciples came to him and he began to teach them, saying,
"Blessed are the humble in spirit, for theirs is the kingdom of heaven.
Blessed are the meek, for they shall inherit the earth.
Blessed are those who mourn now, for they shall be comforted.
Blessed are those who weep now, for they shall laugh.
Blessed are those who hunger and thirst after

righteousness, for they shall be filled.

Blessed are the merciful, for they shall receive mercy.

Blessed are the pure in heart, for they shall see God.

Blessed are the peacemakers, for they shall be called the children of God.

Blessed are those who are persecuted for righteousness' sake, for theirs is the Kingdom of God.

Blessed are you when people insult you, persecute you and falsely say all kinds of evil against you because of me. Rejoice and be glad, because your reward will be great in heaven, for in the same way they persecuted the prophets before you.

You are the salt of the earth, but if the salt loses its flavor how can it be made salty again? It is no longer good for anything, except to be thrown out and trampled.

You are the light of the world. A city on a hill cannot be hidden. Neither do people light a candle and put it under a bushel. Instead, they put it on a candlestick and it gives out light to all who are in the house. Let your light shine before all others, so that they may see your good works and glorify God.

Do not think that I have come to destroy the Law or the prophets. I have not come to destroy, but to fulfill. Verily I say to you that until heaven and earth pass away, not the smallest letter or the least stroke of a pen will in any way disappear from the Law until everything is fulfilled.

Anyone who breaks one of the least of these commandments and teaches others to do the same will be called least in the kingdom of heaven, but whoever keeps and teaches these commandments will be called great in the kingdom of heaven.

I tell you that unless your righteousness surpasses that of the Pharisees and Sadducees, you will not enter into the kingdom of heaven.

You have heard that it was said to the people long ago, 'Do not murder, and whoever commits murder will be in danger of the judgment.' But I say to you that whoever is angry with his brother without a cause will be in danger of the judgment, and whoever says to his brother or sister, 'Raca' will be in danger of the council, but whoever says, 'You fool!' will be in danger of the hell-fire.

Therefore, if you bring a gift to the altar, and while there remember you have something against your brother or sister, you should leave your gift before the altar and go and be reconciled with your brother or sister, and then return to the altar and offer your gift.

Agree with your adversary quickly, before the

adversary delivers you to the judge, and the judge delivers you to the officers and you are thrown into prison. Verily, I tell you the truth. You will not be freed from there until you have paid the last penny.

You have heard it has been said by the prophets, 'Do not commit adultery.' But I say to you that whoever looks upon a woman with lust has already committed adultery with her in his heart. If your right eye causes you to sin, then pluck it out. It is better to enter heaven with one eye than to have the whole body thrown into hell. Further, if your right hand causes you to sin, then cut it off. It is better to enter heaven with one hand than to have the whole body thrown into hell.

Again, you have heard the prophets say, 'Do not break your oaths, but keep the oaths you have made to God.' But I say to you, do not swear at all, either by heaven, for it is God's throne, or by the earth, for it is his footstool, or by Jerusalem, for it is the city of the Great King. Do not swear by your head, for you cannot make even one hair white or black. Simply let your 'yes' be 'yes' and your 'no' be 'no.' Anything beyond this comes from the evil one.

You have heard it said by the prophets, 'An eye for an eye, and a tooth for a tooth.' But I tell you that you should not resist an evil person. If someone strikes you on the right cheek, then turn to him the other also. And if someone wants to sue you and take your coat, let him have your cloak as well. And if someone forces you to go with him one mile, then go with him two miles. Give to whoever asks you and do not turn away the one who wishes to borrow from you.

You have heard it said by the prophets, 'Love your friends and hate your enemies.' But I say to you to love your enemies, bless those who curse you, do good to those who hate you and pray for those who use you and persecute you. In this way you will be the children of God, for God makes the sun to rise on the evil and the good, and sends the rain on the just and on the unjust. If you love only those who love you, what reward do you have? Do not even the Pharisees and tax collectors do this? And if you only welcome your family, do not even the Pharisees and tax collectors do this? Therefore be perfect, even as God in heaven is perfect.

Be careful that you do not perform alms before others, in order to be seen by them. Otherwise, you have no reward in heaven. Therefore, when you perform alms do not sound a trumpet as the hypocrites do in the synagogues and in the streets, so that they may obtain the glory of others. I tell you the truth; they have already received their reward. Instead, when you perform alms, let not your left hand know what the right hand is doing, so that your almsgiving may be in secret. God will see what you do in secret and will reward you openly.

And when you pray do not pray like the hypocrites. They love to pray standing in the synagogues and on the street corners, so that others may see them. I tell you the truth; they have already received their reward. Instead, when you pray, you should enter into your room and shut the door. Pray to God in secret and God, upon hearing your prayers in secret, will reward you openly. When you pray, do not use vain repetitions as the hypocrites do, for they think they will be heard for their many words. Do not be like them, because God already knows what you need even before you ask. Therefore, in this manner you should pray:
'God in heaven,
Hallowed be your name.
Your kingdom come,
Your will be done,
On earth as it is in heaven.
Give us today our daily bread,
And forgive us of our trespasses,
As we forgive those who trespass against us.

The Gospel of Jesus the Christ

Lead us not into temptation,
But deliver us from the evil one,
For yours is the kingdom and the power and the glory
forever, Amen.'

If you forgive others of their trespasses then God
will also forgive you of your trespasses, but if you do
not forgive others then God will not forgive you.

Moreover, when you fast do not be of a sad
countenance like the hypocrites. They disfigure their
faces so that they may appear to fast in front of others.
I tell you the truth; they have already received their
reward. Instead, when you fast, anoint your head and
wash your face, so that you do not appear to fast in
front of others, but only to God, which is in secret. And
God, upon seeing you in secret, will reward you openly.

Do not store up treasures for yourselves on earth,
where moths and rust will destroy them and where
thieves can break in and steal. Instead, lay up for
yourselves treasures in heaven, where neither moths nor
rust can destroy them and where thieves cannot break
in and steal. For where your treasure is, there will your
heart be also.

The light of the body is the eye. If your eye is single
then your whole body will be full of light. But if your
eye is evil then your whole body will be full of darkness.

The Gospel of Jesus the Christ

No one can serve two masters. Either he will hate the one and love the other, or he will hold to the one and despise the other. You cannot serve both God and Mammon.

Therefore, I say to you that you should take no thought for your life, what you will eat or what you will wear. Isn't the life more than food, and the body more than clothing? Look at the birds in the air! They do not sow, neither do they reap or gather into barns. Yet, God takes care of them. Are you not more precious than they? Which one of you by worrying can add a single hour to his life?

And why do you concern yourselves with clothing? Consider the lilies of the fields, how they grow. They toil not, neither do they spin, and yet I say to you that even Solomon in all his glory was not arrayed like one of these. If God so clothes the grass of the field, which is here today and tomorrow is thrown into the oven, shall he not much more clothe you?

Therefore, take no thought, saying, 'what will we eat?' or, 'what will we drink?' or, 'what will we wear?' because God already knows you have need of all these things. Seek first the kingdom of heaven and all these things will be added to you. Therefore, do not worry about tomorrow because tomorrow will take care of itself.

Do not judge others or you also will be judged, and with the same measure that you mete it will be measured back to you. Why do you notice the speck of dust that is in your brother's eye, but do not consider the mote that is in your own eye? How can you say to your brother, 'Let me pull out the mote that is in your eye' but not consider the speck that is in your own eye? First, you must remove the speck that is in your eye, then you can see clearly to remove the mote in your brother's eye.

Who among you shall have a friend to whom you go at midnight saying, 'Friend, lend me three loaves of bread, for a friend of mine has come to visit me and I have nothing for him to eat.' And your friend should answer, 'Don't bother me. The children are in bed and I cannot get up to give it to you.' I say to you that because he is a friend, he will get up and give to you as many loaves as you need.

And I say to you, ask and it will be given to you; seek and you will find; knock and it will be opened to you. For everyone that asks will receive, everyone that seeks will find and to everyone that knocks, it will be opened. What kind of parent are you that, if his child asks for bread, will give him a stone? Or, if he asks for a fish, will give him a snake? If you then, though you are evil, know how to give good gifts to your children, how much more will God give good things to those who ask?

Do unto others, as you would have them do unto you, for this sums up the Law and the prophets.

You must enter through the narrow gate, for wide is the gate and broad is the way that leads to destruction, and many will go down that path. But straight is the gate and narrow is the way that leads to eternal life, and only a few will find it.

Beware of false prophets, which come to you in sheep's clothing but inside are like ravenous wolves. You will know them by their fruits. Do people gather grapes of thorns or figs of thistles? A good tree cannot bear bad fruit, and a corrupt tree cannot bear good fruit. Every tree that bears bad fruit will be cut down and thrown into the fire. Therefore, you will recognize them by their fruits.

Not everyone who says to me, 'Lord, Lord' will enter into the kingdom of heaven, but only those who do the will of God. Many people will say to me on that day, 'Lord, have we not prophesied in your name? We have cast out demons in your name, and in your name we have done wonderful works.' And I will say to them, *'Get away from me, for I never knew you.'*

Therefore, whoever hears these teachings and acts accordingly will be like a wise man who built his house upon a rock. The rain descended and the floods came, and the wind blew and beat upon that house. Yet, it did not fall because it was founded on a rock.

Everyone who hears these teachings and does not act accordingly will be like a foolish man who built his house upon the sand. The rain descended and the floods came, and the winds blew and beat upon that house. That house fell, and great was the fall of it!"

After Jesus had finished speaking all the people were astounded because he taught them as one with authority, unlike the scribes.

Jesus Begins To Heal The Sick

After Jesus came down from the mountain great multitudes followed him. A leper came to Jesus and said, "Lord, if you will, you can make me clean." Jesus reached out his hand and said, *"I will, be clean!"* Immediately the man's leprosy was cleansed. Then Jesus said to him, *"Don't tell anyone. Go and show yourself to the priests and offer the alms that Moses commanded as a testimony to them."*

When Jesus entered Capernaum a centurion came to him and said, "Lord, my servant lies at home tormented and sick with the palsy."

Jesus said to him, *"I will come and heal him."* The centurion replied, "Lord, I am not worthy to have you under my roof, but speak the words only and my servant will be healed."

When Jesus heard this he marveled and said to the crowd, *"I tell you the truth, I have not found anyone in all of Israel with such great faith! And I say to you that many will come from the East and the West and will sit down with Abraham, Isaac and Jacob in the kingdom of heaven, but the children who do not believe will be thrown out into the darkness, where there will be weeping and gnashing of teeth."* Then Jesus said to the centurion, *"Go your way, and it will be done just as you have believed."* And his servant was healed that very hour.

When Jesus came to Peter's house he saw that Peter's mother-in-law lay sick with a fever. Jesus touched her hand and the fever left her. Then she got up and began to attend on them. That evening the people brought many who were possessed with demons, and Jesus cast out the spirits with his word and he healed all their sick.

Thus the prophecy was fulfilled, which was spoken by the prophet Isaiah, "He took our infirmities and carried our sicknesses."

Now, when Jesus saw great multitudes following him, he and his disciples left for the other side of the shore. A certain scribe came to Jesus and said, "Master, I will follow you wherever you go." Jesus said to him, *"The foxes have holes and the birds of the air have nests, but the Son of Man has no place to rest his head."*

Another of his disciples said to Jesus, "Let me first go and bury my father." Jesus said, *"Follow me, and let the dead bury the dead."*

When Jesus had passed over to the other side of the shore he was brought a man who was sick with the palsy. Jesus said to him, *"Son, be of good cheer, your sins are forgiven."*

Some of the scribes said within themselves, "This man blasphemes." Jesus, knowing their thoughts, said to them, *"Which is easier to say, 'your sins are forgiven' or 'get up and walk'? So that you may know that the Son of Man has power on earth to forgive sins I say 'Arise, take up your bed and go home.'"*

Then the man with the palsy got up and went into his house. When the multitude saw this they marveled and glorified God.

Jesus Teaches Using Parables

Jesus began again to teach by the seaside. There was a great multitude gathered there, so he entered into a boat and sat in the sea while the whole multitude gathered on the shore.

Jesus taught them many things using parables, and he said to them, "Listen! *A farmer went out to sow his seeds. And it came to pass, as he sowed, some fell by the wayside and the birds of the air came and devoured those seeds. And some seeds fell on stony ground where there was not much soil, and immediately those seeds sprang up because there was no depth of earth. But when the sun came up those plants were scorched, and because they had no root they withered away. And some of the seeds fell among thorns and the thorns grew around them and they yielded no fruit. Some other seeds fell on good ground, and these seeds did produce fruit that sprang up and increased, some by thirty-fold, some by sixty-fold and some by a hundred-fold. Those with ears, let them* hear!"

The disciples came to Jesus and asked, "Why do you speak to them in parables?"

Jesus said to them, *"It has been given to you to know the mystery of the Kingdom of God, but to others it must be delivered in parables because they see but do not perceive, and they hear but do not understand. And in them the prophecy of Isaiah is fulfilled, 'By hearing you shall hear and shall not understand, and by seeing you shall see and shall not perceive.' For this people's heart is callous and their ears are dull of hearing, and they have closed their eyes. But at some point they might be converted and I would heal them.*

Blessed are your eyes because they see, and blessed are your ears because they hear. Verily I say to you, that many prophets and righteous men have desired to see those things that you see and have not seen them, and hear those things that you hear and have not heard them. Listen, therefore, to the meaning of this parable.

The seed that was sown is the Word. Those that were sown by the wayside are the ones who hear the Word and do not understand it. Then the devil immediately comes and takes away the Word that was sown in their hearts. The ones that were sown

on stony ground are those who, when they hear the
Word, immediately receive it with joy. But they
have no root in themselves and therefore endure for
only a short time. Afterward, when affliction and
persecution arises for the Word's sake, they are immediately offended. And the ones that were sown among
the thorns are those who hear the Word but the cares
of this world, the deceitfulness of riches and the lusts
for other things enter in, choking the Word, and it does
not become fruitful. The ones that were sown on good
ground are those who hear the Word, receive it and
bear fruit, some thirty-fold, some sixty-fold and some
a hundred-fold.

The kingdom of heaven is like a man who sows
seed in the ground and then sleeps. It rises day and
night as the seed grows, and he does not know how.
The earth brings forth fruit from herself; first the
blade, then the ear and then the full corn in the ear.
And when the fruit has come the man puts the sickle
into it, because the harvest is ready.

The kingdom of heaven is like leaven, which a
woman took and hid in three measures of meal, and
the whole loaf was leavened.

How shall we compare the kingdom of heaven? It
is like a grain of mustard seed, which, when sown into

the earth, is the smallest of all seeds, but when it grows up it is greater than all the other herbs. It shoots out great branches, so that the birds of the air may lodge in its shadow."

Jesus spoke to the multitudes in parables and when they were alone, he explained all the meanings to his disciples. Thus it was fulfilled that which was spoken by the prophet, "I will open my mouth in parables; I will utter things which have been kept secret from the foundation of the world."

Someone in the crowd said to Jesus, "Master, speak to my brother, so that he will divide his inheritance with me."

Jesus said, *"Sir, who made me a judge or divider over you?"* Then Jesus said to the multitude,

"Beware of covetousness! A person's life does not consist of the abundance of his possessions."

Jesus told another parable, saying,

"The ground of a certain rich man brought forth very plentifully. The man thought within himself, 'What shall I do, because I have no room to store all of my fruits?' And he said, 'This I will do: I will tear down my barns and build bigger ones, and there I will store all of my fruits and possessions. And I will say to my

soul, *"Soul, you have vast stores of goods laid up for many years. Take your leisure, eat, drink and be merry." '*

But God said to him, 'You fool! Tonight your soul will be required of you, and then what will you do with all of your fruits and possessions?' So shall it be for those who lay up treasure for themselves, but are not rich toward God."

After they had sent the crowds away, a great storm began on the sea and the waves beat upon their boat. Jesus was in the back of the boat, asleep on a pillow. His disciples came and woke him saying, "Master, save us!" Jesus replied, *"Why are you afraid, O you of little faith?"* Then Jesus rebuked the winds and the waves saying, *"Peace, be still!"* At once the wind ceased and there was a great calm. The disciples were amazed and asked, "What kind of man is this, that even the wind and the sea obeys him?"

Jesus Continues To Heal The Sick

Jesus and his disciples crossed over the river to the other shore and into the country of the Gergesenes. As Jesus was passing through that country he saw a man named Matthew sitting at the tax collector's booth and he said to him, *"Come and follow me."* Matthew immediately got up and followed Jesus.

And it came to pass, as Jesus sat down to eat, many publicans and sinners came and sat down with him and his disciples. When the Pharisees saw this they asked his disciples, "Why does your Master eat with publicans and sinners?"

When Jesus heard this he said to them, *"The well have no need of a physician, but only the sick. Go and learn what this means: 'I desire mercy and not sacrifice.' I have not come to call the righteous, but sinners to repentance."*

The disciples of John the Baptist came to Jesus and asked, "Why do we and the Pharisees fast often, but your disciples do not fast?" Jesus answered them, *"Can the children in the bride chamber mourn as long as the bridegroom is with them? The days will come when the bridegroom will be taken from them, and then they will fast."*

While Jesus was speaking a certain ruler came to him and said, "My daughter is dead, but come and lay your hands on her so that she may live." Jesus and his disciples got up and followed the man.

As they were walking, a woman who had been diseased with an issue of blood for twelve years came behind Jesus and touched the hem of his garment saying to herself, "If I only touch his robe I will be healed."

Jesus turned around and said to the woman, *"Daughter, be of good cheer! Your faith has made you whole."* And the woman was healed that very hour.

When Jesus came into the ruler's house he saw the minstrels and the people paying their respects. Jesus said to them, *"Give peace, the maiden is not dead but asleep."* After everyone had left the room Jesus took the girl by the hand and she got up out of the bed. The fame of this act became known throughout the lands.

Jesus went into all the cities and villages, teaching in the synagogues and preaching the gospel of the kingdom. And he healed every sickness and disease among the people.

When he saw the crowds, Jesus was moved with compassion because they were scattered about, like sheep without a shepherd. Then Jesus said to his disciples, *"The harvest is plentiful, but the laborers are few. Pray, therefore, to the Lord of the harvest, that he may bring more laborers into the field."*

Jesus Sends Out His Disciples

Jesus appointed seventy followers to be disciples and he sent them out two by two into every city and place where he himself would go.

He instructed them saying, *"Do not go to the Gentiles or into any city of the Samaritans, but instead go to the lost sheep of the House of Israel. As you go, preach saying, 'The kingdom of heaven is at hand.'*

Heal the sick, cleanse the lepers, raise the dead and cast out demons. Freely you have been given, so freely you should give.

Do not take gold, or silver, or brass, or money for your journey, neither two coats, neither shoes nor staffs, for the workman is worthy of his keep.

Whatever city or town you enter, inquire who in that city is worthy, and there you should stay until you leave. When you enter a house you should bless it, and if the house is worthy then let your peace enter into it. But if the house is not worthy, then when you leave that house or city you should shake off the dust from your feet. I tell you the truth that it will be more tolerable for Sodom and Gomorra on the Day of Judgement than for that city.

Behold, I send you out as sheep among wolves! Therefore, be as wise as a serpent and as harmless as a dove.

Beware of men, because they will deliver you to the councils and they will chastise you in their synagogues. You will be brought before governors and kings for my sake, but when they deliver you up take no thought about how you will answer because it will be given to you what you will speak. It is not you who will speak, but the Holy Spirit will speak through you.

When they persecute you in one city, then flee into another. The disciple is not above his Master, nor the servant above the Lord. It is enough that the disciple be as his own master. Do not fear them, because there is nothing covered that will not be revealed and nothing hidden that will not be known.

What I tell to you in the darkness you should speak in the light. And what you hear with your ears you should preach upon the housetops.

Do not fear those who can kill the body but not the soul. But rather, fear the evil one who is able to destroy both body and soul in hell.

Are not two sparrows sold for a penny? And not

even one of these will fall to the ground without God's knowledge. Do not fear, therefore, you are worth more than many sparrows. Why, even the very hairs on your head are all numbered.

Whoever confesses me before men, those I will confess before my Father, which is in heaven. But whoever denies me before men, those also I will deny before my Father.

Do not think that I have come to bring peace upon the earth, for I have not come to bring peace, but a sword. For I have come to set a man against his father, and the daughter against her mother, and the daughter-in-law against her mother-in-law. A person's enemies will be from his own household. Those who love their father or mother more than me are not worthy of me, and those who love their daughter or son more than me are not worthy of me. The one who does not take his cross and follow me is not worthy of me. The one who finds his own life will lose it, and the one who loses his own life for my sake will find it.

Those who receive you receive me, and those who receive me receive the One who sent me. Those who receive a prophet in the name of a prophet will receive a prophet's reward, and those who receive a righteous man in the name of a righteous man will receive a *righteous man's reward. And whoever gives even a drink of a cup of cold water to one of these little ones in the name of a disciple will not lose his reward."*

Afterward the seventy returned again with joy, saying, "Lord, even the devils are subject unto us through your name." Jesus said to them, *"I watched as Satan fell from heaven like lightning. Behold, I give you power to walk on snakes and scorpions, and I give you power over the enemy. Nothing will be able to harm you.*

Nevertheless, do not rejoice because the spirits are subject unto you, but rather rejoice because your names are written in heaven."

Jesus Continues Preaching The Doctrine

After Jesus had finished instructing his disciples he departed from there and went to teach and preach in their cities.

Now, when John the Baptist heard, while he was in prison about the works of the Christ, he sent two of his disciples to ask Jesus, "Are you the One who is to come or should we look for another?"

Jesus answered them, *"Go and tell John again*

what you have seen and heard. The blind receive sight, the lame walk, the lepers are cleansed, the deaf hear, the dead are raised up and the good news of the gospel is preached to the poor. Blessed is the one who is not offended by me."

As John's disciples departed, Jesus said to the multitudes concerning John, *"What did you go out into the wilderness to see, a reed shaken by the wind? What did you go out to see, a man clothed in soft raiment? What did you go out to see, a prophet? I tell you the truth, he is much more than a prophet. This is the one of whom it is written: 'Behold! I send a messenger before you, who shall prepare your way.' Verily I say to you that there is none born of women that is greater than John the Baptist. Nevertheless, the one who is least in the kingdom of heaven is greater than he.*

From the days of John the Baptist until now the kingdom of heaven has been advancing forcefully. All the prophets and the Law prophesied until John. And if you can accept it, this is Elijah, who was to come before me. Those with ears, let them hear.

How shall I compare this generation? It is like little children sitting in the marketplace and calling out to their fellows and saying, 'We have piped for you and you did not dance. We have mourned for you and you have not lamented.' For John came neither eating nor drinking and they say of him, 'He has a devil.' The Son of Man came eating and drinking and they say, 'Look! A glutton and a friend to publicans and sinners!' "

A Pharisee Invites Jesus To Dinner

At that time one of the Pharisees invited Jesus to eat dinner at his house. Jesus went with Simon, the Pharisee, and sat down to eat.

A woman, who lived in the city, heard that Jesus was having dinner at Simon's house. She went to his house and brought an alabaster box of precious ointment. Then she stood at Jesus' feet behind him weeping, and she began to wash his feet with her tears. She wiped them with the hairs of her head and kissed his feet, and she anointed his feet with the ointment.

Now, when the Pharisee saw this he said within himself, "This man, if he were truly a prophet, would have known who and what manner of woman this is that touches him, for she is a prostitute."

Jesus said to him, *"Simon, I have something to say to you."* Simon answered, "Say on." Jesus said, *"There was a certain creditor who had two debtors. One of the debtors owed him five hundred pence and the other owed him fifty pence. When they could not pay him, he frankly forgave them both. Tell me, therefore, which of those two will love him the most?"*

Simon answered Jesus, "I suppose the one to whom he forgave the most." Jesus said, *"You have rightly judged."*

Then Jesus turned to the woman and said to Simon, *"Do you see this woman here? When I came into your house you gave me no water for my feet, but this woman has washed my feet with her tears and wiped them with the hairs of her head. You did not anoint my head with oil, but this woman has anointed my feet with ointment. Therefore I say to you that her sins, which are many, are forgiven because she has loved much. But those to whom little is forgiven, the same will love little."* Then Jesus said to the woman, *"Your sins are forgiven."* The people who were sitting at the dinner table began to say among themselves, "Who is this that forgives sins also?" Jesus said to the woman, *"Your faith has saved you, go in peace."*

The Gospel of Jesus the Christ

Jesus Speaks With Nicodemus

After these things Jesus and his disciples went to the land of Judea. There was a certain man of the Pharisees named Nicodemus, a ruler of the Jews. Nicodemus came to Jesus at night and said to him, "Rabbi, we know that you are a teacher sent by God, because no one could do these miracles that you do unless God is with him." Jesus answered and said to him, *"Verily I say to you that unless a man is born again, he cannot see the Kingdom of God."*

Nicodemus asked him, "How can a man be born again when he is old? Can he enter a second time into his mother's womb and be born again?"

Jesus said, *"Verily, verily, I say to you that unless someone is born of water and of the Spirit, he cannot enter into the Kingdom of God. That which is born of the flesh is flesh, and that which is born of the Spirit is Spirit.*

Marvel not that I say to you, 'You must be born again.' The wind blows wherever it pleases and you can hear its sound, but cannot tell where it comes from or where it goes. So it is also with everyone who is born of the Spirit."

Nicodemus asked, "How can these things be?" Jesus answered him and said, "*Are not you a master of Israel, and you do not know these things? I say to you that we speak of what we know and testify of that which we have seen, and you have not received our witness. If I have told you of earthly things and you have not believed, then how shall you believe if I tell you of heavenly things?*

No man has ascended up to heaven except he that came down from heaven, even the Son of Man. And as Moses lifted up the serpent in the wilderness, even so must the Son of Man be lifted up; so that whosoever believes in him shall not perish, but shall have eternal life.

God did not send his Son into the world to condemn the world, but that the world through him might be saved.

The one who believes on me is not condemned, but the one who does not believe is condemned already. And this is the condemnation: light has come into the world, and men loved darkness rather than light because their deeds were evil.

Everyone who commits evil hates the light and does not come to the light, lest his deeds should be reproved.

But those who do good come into the light, so that their deeds are made manifest and are right in God."

Jesus Speaks With The Woman Of Samaria

Jesus and his disciples left Judea and departed into Galilee. As they traveled they had to pass through Samaria. They came to a city of Samaria called Sychar, near the parcel of ground that Jacob gave to his son Joseph.

Now, Jacob's well was there and Jesus sat on the well while his disciples went into the city to buy meat. A woman of Samaria came to draw water from the well and Jesus said to her, *"Give me a drink."* The woman of Samaria said to him, "How is it that you, being a Jew, ask me, a Samaritan, to give you a drink? The Jews have no dealings with the Samaritans."

Jesus answered and said to her, *"If you knew of the gift of God and whom it is that said to you, 'Give me a drink' then you would have asked of him and he would have given you living water."*

The woman said, "Sir, you have nothing to draw with and the well is deep. Where would You get this living water? Are you greater than our father Jacob, who gave us the well?"

Jesus answered her and said, *"Whoever drinks of this water will thirst again, but whoever drinks of the water that I shall give him will never thirst. For the water that I shall give him shall be a well of water springing into everlasting life."*

The woman said, "Sir, give me this water, so that I will never thirst again." Jesus said to her, *"Go and call your husband, and then come here."* The woman answered and said, "I have no husband." Jesus said, *"You have rightly said, 'I have no husband' because you have had five husbands and the man you have now is not your husband, in this you have spoken the truth."*

The woman said, "Sir, I perceive you are a prophet. Our fathers worshiped in this mountain, and you say that Jerusalem is the place we ought to worship."

Jesus said to her, *"Woman, believe me, the hour is coming when you shall neither in this mountain, nor at Jerusalem worship God. But the hour comes and now is, when the true worshipers shall worship God in spirit and in truth, for God seeks such to worship him. God is a Spirit, and those who worship him must worship in Spirit and in Truth."*

The woman said, "I know that the Messiah is coming. When he comes he will tell us all things."

Jesus said, *"I am He that speaks to you."* At that time the disciples returned and marveled when they saw Jesus talking to the woman.

The woman then left her water pot and went her way into the city. She said to everyone, "Come and see a man who told me everything that I ever did. Is not this the Messiah?" Then they all went out to meet Jesus.

In the meantime his disciples begged Jesus, saying, "Master, eat." Jesus said to them, *"I have meat to eat that you know not of."* The disciples said among themselves, "Has someone brought him something to eat?" Jesus said, *"My meat is to do the will of the One who sent me, and to finish his work. Do you say, 'There are four more months and then the harvest is ready?' Behold, I say to you to lift up your eyes and look upon the fields, for they are white already to harvest.*

He that reaps receives wages, and gathers fruit into eternal life. Then he who sows and he who reaps will rejoice together. Therefore, this saying is true, 'One sows, and another reaps.' I have sent you to reap where you have not sown."

And many of the Samaritans believed on Jesus because of what the woman testified, "He told me everything I ever did." So, when the Samaritans had come to him, they asked Jesus to stay with them, and he stayed there two days.

Then many Samaritans said to the woman, "Now we believe, not because of what you told us but because we have heard his words ourselves and know that this is indeed the Messiah, the Savior of the world." After two days Jesus and his disciples left from there and went into Galilee.

Jesus Criticizes The Cities Where He Preached

Jesus began to criticize the cities where most of his miracles had been performed because they did not repent, *"Woe to you, Chorazin! Woe to you, Bethsaida! For if the mighty works, which were done in you, had been done in Tyre and Sidon, they would have repented long ago. I say to you that it will be more tolerable for Tyre and Sidon on the Day of Judgment than for you.*

And you, Capernaum, will you be exalted unto heaven? No, you shall be brought down into hell. For if the mighty works that have been done in you had been done in Sodom it would have remained to this day. I say to you that it will be more tolerable for the land of Sodom on the Day of Judgment than for you.

I thank you, God, Lord of the heavens and the earth, because you have hid these things from the wise and prudent, and have revealed them unto babes. Even so Lord, for it was your good pleasure.

My Father reveals all things to me, and no one knows the Son except the Father. And no one knows the Father except the Son, and those to whom the Son chooses to reveal him.

Come to me, all of you who labor and are heavy laden, and I will give you rest. Take my yoke upon you and learn from me, for I am meek and humble in heart, and you shall find rest within your souls. My yoke is easy and my burden is light."

The Son Of Man Is Lord Of The Sabbath

At that time Jesus and his disciples went through the cornfields on the Sabbath day. His disciples were hungry and plucked the ears of corn and began to eat them. Some of the Pharisees said to him, "Look! Your disciples do that which is not lawful to do on the Sabbath day." Jesus said to them, *"Have you not read what David did when he and those who were with him were hungry; how he entered into the house of God and ate the bread offered to God, which was not lawful for him and those who were with him to eat? Or, have you never read in the law, how that on the Sabbath days the priests in the temple profane the Sabbath, and are blameless? But I say to you that in this place there is One who is greater than the temple. If you had known what this means, 'I desire mercy and not sacrifice' then you would not have condemned the guiltless. For the Son of Man is Lord even of the Sabbath day."*

Jesus Heals On The Sabbath Day

After Jesus left from there he went into the synagogue and a man with a withered hand was there. Looking for an excuse to accuse Jesus, the Pharisees asked him, "Is it lawful to heal on the Sabbath?"

Jesus said to them, *"If you have one sheep and it falls into a pit on the Sabbath day, who among you will not lay hold of it and lift it out of the pit? How much more value is a man than a sheep? Therefore, it is lawful to do good works on the Sabbath day."*

Jesus said to the man, *"Stretch out your hand."* The man stretched out his hand and it was made whole, just like the other. Jesus said to them, *"My Father works, and so I likewise work."*

Therefore the Jews sought even more to kill Jesus, because he not only had broken the Sabbath but also had said that God was his Father, making himself equal with God.

Then Jesus said to them, *"Verily, verily, I say to you that the Son can do nothing of himself, but he does what he sees the Father do, for the things the Father does, so likewise does the Son.*

The Father loves the Son and shows him all things. And he will show him greater things than these, so that you may marvel. For even as God raises up the dead and quickens them, so also the Son quickens whom he will.

God judges no one, but has committed all judgment to the Son. All men should honor the Son, even as they honor the Father. The one who does not honor the Son, the same does not honor the Father, which has sent him. Verily, I say to you that the one who hears my Word and believes on the One that sent me has everlasting life, and shall not come into condemnation, but is passed from death into life.

The hour is coming, and now is, when the dead shall hear the voice of the Son of God, and they that hear shall live.

I can do nothing by myself. As I hear, I judge. My judgment is just, because I do not seek after my own will, but the will of God.

If I bear witness of myself, my witness is not true. There is another who bears witness of me, and I know that his witness is true. You went to John and he bore witness to the Truth. He was a burning and a shining light, and you were willing for a season to rejoice in his light.

I have greater witness than that of John, for the works that God has given me to finish, those works that I do bear witness that God has sent me. And God himself, which has sent me, has borne witness of me. You have never heard his voice nor seen his shape. And those of you who do not believe the One who he has sent do not have God's Word abiding in you.

Search the scriptures, for in them you think you have eternal life, and they testify of me. You will not come to me, so that you may have eternal life. I do not seek honor from men. But I know that you do not have the love of God in you. I have come in my Father's *name and you do not receive me. If another shall come in his own name, him you will receive.*

How can you believe, you who seek honor from one another and do not seek the honor that comes only from God? Do not think that I will accuse you to God. There is one who accuses you, even Moses in whom you trust. If you believe Moses you would believe me, because he wrote of me. But if you do not believe his writings, then how will you believe my words?"

Then the Pharisees went out and held a meeting, and they tried to devise a plan to destroy Jesus. Jesus knew their thoughts and departed from there.

The Pharisees Ask For A Sign From Jesus

Great multitudes followed Jesus and he healed all the sick among them. All the people were amazed and said, "Isn't this the Son of David?" When the Pharisees heard this they said, "It is only by Beelzebub, the prince of demons, that this fellow casts out demons."

Jesus said to them, *"Any kingdom divided against itself will be destroyed, and every city or house divided against itself will not stand. If Satan drives out Satan,* then he is divided against himself. How then can his kingdom stand? If I drive out demons by Beelzebub, then by whom do your children drive them out? Therefore, they will be your judges. But if I cast out demons by the Spirit of God, then the Kingdom of God has come upon you.

How can someone enter a strong man's house and rob him of his possessions, unless he first ties up the strong man? Those who are not with me are against me, and those who do not gather with me scatter.

Therefore, I say to you that all manner of sin and blasphemy will be forgiven, except blasphemy against the Holy Spirit will not be forgiven. Whoever speaks evil against the Son of Man will be forgiven, but whoever speaks evil against the Holy Spirit will not be forgiven, neither in this world nor in the world to come.

Either make the tree good and the fruit will be good, or make the tree bad and the fruit will be bad. The tree is known by its fruit.

O generation of vipers! How can you, being evil, speak good things? A good person, out of the good treasure in his heart, speaks good things, but an evil person, out of the evil in his heart, speaks bad things. The mouth speaks out of the overflow of the heart. I say to you that, on the Day of Judgment, people will *account for every idle word they have spoken. By your words you will be acquitted, and by your words you will be condemned."*

Some of the scribes and Pharisees said to Jesus, "Master, we would like to see a sign from you." Jesus answered them, saying, *"When it is evening you say, 'It will be fair weather because the sky is red.' And in the morning you say, 'It will be foul weather because the sky is red and lowering.' You hypocrites! You can discern the face of the sky, but can you discern the signs of the times? An evil and adulterous generation seeks after a sign but there will be no sign given, except the sign of the prophet Jonas. For as he was in the belly of the fish for three days and three nights, so shall the Son of Man be three days and three nights in the heart of the earth.*

The people of Nineveh will rise up in judgment against this generation and shall condemn it because they repented at the preaching of Jonas, and now One who is greater than Jonas is here.

The Queen of the South will rise up in judgment against this generation and condemn it, for she came from the uttermost parts of the earth to hear the wisdom of Solomon and now One who is greater than Solomon has come.

The Gospel of Jesus the Christ

When the unclean spirit has gone out of a man it walks through arid places and does not find rest. Then it says to itself, 'I will return to the place where I came from.' When it returns to that place it finds it empty, swept clean and put in order. Then it goes and gets seven other spirits more wicked than itself and together they enter into that place and they live there. The state of that man is even worse than before. That is how it will be with this evil generation."

While Jesus was preaching to the people someone said, "Look! Your mother and brothers are outside wanting to speak with you."

Jesus asked them, *"Who is my mother? And who are my brothers?"* Then he reached out his hand toward his disciples and said, *"Behold, my mother and my brothers! For whoever does the will of God in heaven is my mother, brother and sister."*

The Parable Of The Weeds

That same day Jesus went out of the house and sat by the seaside. A great crowd followed him and he spoke many things to them using parables, saying, *"The kingdom of heaven is like a man who sowed good seeds in his field, but while the* man slept his enemy came and sowed weeds among the wheat and then went his way.

When the blade sprang up and began to bear its fruit the weeds appeared with it. The servants of the householder came and said to him, 'Sir, didn't you sow good seeds in your field? Why are there weeds in the field?' The householder said to them, 'An enemy has done this.' The servants said to him, 'Shall we go and gather up the weeds?' He answered, 'No, if you gather up the weeds now you might root up the wheat with them. Let them grow together until the harvest. At the time of the harvest I will tell the reapers to gather the weeds and bind them in bundles and burn them. Then I will tell them to gather the wheat and bring it into my barn.' "

Then Jesus sent the crowd away and went into the house with his disciples. His disciples came to him and said, "Master, explain the parable of the weeds to us."

Jesus said to them, "The one that sows the good seed is the Son of Man. The field is the world. The good seed are the children of God, but the weeds are the children of Satan. The enemy that sowed them is the devil. The harvest is the end of the world and the reapers are the angels. Therefore, as the weeds are

235

gathered and burned in the fire, so shall it be at the end of the world. The Son of Man will send out his angels and they will gather out of the kingdom all things that cause sin and all who do evil. They will throw them into the fiery furnace where there will be weeping and gnashing of teeth. Then the righteous and good will shine with radiance in the Kingdom of God. Those with ears, let them hear.

The kingdom of heaven is like treasure hidden in a field. When someone found it, he went and sold all that he owned and bought that field.

Again, the kingdom of heaven is like a merchant seeking fine pearls. When he finds one of great value he goes and sells all that he has so that he can buy it.

Again, the kingdom of heaven is like a net which, when cast into the sea, brought up every kind of fish. When it was full it was drawn up to shore. Then the fishermen sat down and gathered the good fish into baskets, but they threw the bad fish away. So shall it be at the end of the world. The angels will come and sever the wicked from the just, and will throw the wicked into the fiery furnace."

Jesus asked his disciples, *"Have you understood all these things?"* They replied to him, "Yes, Lord." Then Jesus said to them, *"Therefore, every teacher of*

The Gospel of Jesus the Christ

*the Law who has been instructed about the kingdom of
heaven is like a householder who brings out of his
house new treasures as well as old."*

Jesus Goes To Nazareth

After Jesus had preached these parables he
left from there and went into his own country
called Nazareth. As was the custom, he went into
the synagogue on the Sabbath day and stood up
to read. He was given the book of the prophet
Isaiah and when he opened the book he spoke,
*"The Spirit of the Lord is upon me because he has
anointed me to preach the gospel to the poor. He has
sent me to heal the brokenhearted, to preach deliverance to the captives, to give sight to the blind, to set at
liberty those that are bruised; to preach the acceptable
year of the Lord."* He closed the book and handed
it to the minister, and sat down. The eyes of
everyone there were fastened upon him. Then
Jesus said, *"Today this scripture has been fulfilled in
yours ears."* Everyone wondered at the gracious
words that proceeded out of his mouth and they
said, "Isn't he the carpenter's son? And isn't his
mother called Mary? And aren't his brothers and

sisters here with us? How then is he able to do these mighty works?" They were offended by him.

Jesus said to them, *"You will surely say to me, 'Physician, heal thyself. Whatever we have heard done in Capernaum, do also here in your own country.' Verily I say to you that a prophet is not without honor, except in his own country and among his own family."* And Jesus did not perform many miracles there because of their lack of faith.

Jesus Feeds The Multitude

As he traveled on, Jesus saw a crowd gathered. He was moved with compassion, and he healed all their sick.

When it was evening his disciples came to him and said, "Send the crowds away so that they can go into the villages and get something to eat." Jesus said, *"They do not need to leave. You give them something to eat."* The disciples said, "We have here only five loaves of bread and two fish." Jesus said, *"Bring them here to me."*

Jesus commanded the multitude to sit down on the grass and he took the five loaves of bread and the two fish and, looking up to heaven, he blessed them. Then he gave the loaves to his disciples, and the disciples gave them to the multitude. All of them ate and were filled, and the fragments left over filled twelve baskets. The number that had eaten was about five thousand.

Jesus Warns Of The Teachings Of The Pharisees

When the disciples came to the other side of the shore, they had forgotten to take bread. Jesus said to them, *"Take heed, and beware of the leaven of the Pharisees and Sadducees."* They said among themselves, "He said this because we have taken no bread." Jesus said to them, *"Oh you of little faith, why do you reason among yourselves because you have brought no bread? You still do not understand? Don't you remember the five loaves of bread and five thousand, and how many baskets were left over? How is it that you do not understand that what I spoke to you is not concerning bread, but that you should beware of the leaven of the Pharisees and Sadducees?"* Then the disciples understood that Jesus warned them not about the leaven of bread, but of the teachings of the Pharisees and Sadducees.

The Gospel of Jesus the Christ

Jesus Walks On The Water

Afterwards Jesus commanded his disciples to get into a boat and go ahead of him to the other shore. Then he sent the multitude away. Jesus went up into a mountain to pray. The boat was now in the middle of the sea being tossed by waves because a storm was approaching. In the fourth watch of the night Jesus went out to them, walking on the water. When the disciples saw this they were afraid, saying, "It is a spirit!"

Jesus said to them, *"Do not be afraid, it is I."* Peter called out, "Master, if it is you then command me to come to you on the water." Jesus said, *"Come!"*

When Peter came down out of the boat he walked on the water to go to Jesus, but when he saw the boisterous waves he became afraid and began to sink. He cried out to Jesus, "Master, save me!" Immediately Jesus stretched out his hand and caught Peter and said to him, *"You of little faith, why did you doubt?"*

When they got into the boat the wind stopped. Those who were in the boat came and worshiped Jesus saying, "It is true. You are the

Son of God!"

After they had gone to the other shore they came into the land of Gennesaret. When the people heard that Jesus was among them they went out to meet him and brought all who were diseased to him. They asked Jesus if they may touch his clothes, and all those who touched him were healed.

Jesus Is The Bread Of Life

When the people had found Jesus on the other side of the sea they asked him, "Rabbi, when did you come here?" Jesus answered them, *"Verily, I say to you that you sought me not because you saw the miracles, but because you ate of the loaves of bread and were filled. Do not labor after the meat that perishes, but rather labor after the meat that endures into everlasting life. This is the meat that the Son of Man will give to you."*

Then they asked him, "What shall we do in order that we might work the works of God?" Jesus said, *"This is the work of God: that you believe on the One whom God has sent."* They said to Jesus, "Our fathers did eat manna in the desert as it is written: 'He gave them bread from heaven to eat.'" Jesus said to them, *"Moses did not give you bread from heaven, but my Father has given you the true bread from heaven. For the bread of God is that which comes down from heaven and gives life to the world."*

Then they said, "Lord, evermore give us this bread." Jesus said to them, *"I am the bread of life. The one who comes to me will never hunger, and the one who believes on me will never thirst. All those who God gives to me will come to me, and I will not reject anyone who comes to me. I came down from heaven, not to do my own will, but to do the will of God. And this is God's will: that everyone who sees the Son and believes upon him will have everlasting life, and I will raise him up at the last day."*

The Jews began to murmur because he had said, *"I am the bread that came down from heaven."* They said, "Is not this Jesus, the son of Joseph, whose father and mother we know? How is it then that he says, 'I came down from heaven'?" Jesus answered and said to them, *"Do not murmur among yourselves. No one can come to me unless God draws him to me, and I will lift him up at the last day. It is written by the prophets: 'And they shall all be*

*taught of God.' Everyone, therefore, who has heard
and learned of my Father will come to me.*

*Verily, I say to you, 'The one who believes on me
has everlasting life.' I am that bread of life. Your fathers did eat manna in the wilderness, and are dead.
This is the bread that comes down from heaven, and if
anyone eats thereof, he will not die.*

*I am the living bread that came down from heaven.
If anyone eats of this bread he will live forever. The
bread that I will give him is my flesh, which I will give
for the life of the world. Whoever eats of my flesh and
drinks of my blood has eternal life, and I will raise him
up on the last day."*

Jesus Explains What Defiles A Person

The scribes and the Pharisees came to Jesus
and asked, "Why do your disciples transgress
the tradition of the elders by not washing their
hands before they eat?"

Jesus said to them, *"Why do you transgress the
commandment of God for the sake of your traditions?
God commanded you to honor your mother and father,
but you say that if a man says to his father or mother,
'Whatever help you might otherwise have received is a*

gift devoted to God' he is not to 'honor his father' with it. Thus, you nullify the word of God for the sake of your tradition. You hypocrites! Isaiah was right about you when he said, 'These people honor me with their lips, but their hearts are far from me. Their teachings are only rules taught by men.' "

Jesus called the multitude to him and said, *"Listen and understand! It is not what goes into the mouth that defiles a man, but what comes out of the mouth that defiles a man."*

The disciples said to Jesus, "Did you know that the Pharisees were offended when they heard this?" Jesus answered them and said, *"Every plant that God did not plant will be rooted up. Leave them alone. They are the blind leaders leading the blind. And if the blind lead the blind, then both will fall into the pit."*

Peter said to Jesus, "Explain this parable to us." Jesus said, *"Whatever enters in at the mouth goes into the belly and is cast out of the body, but the things that come out of the mouth come out of the heart. For out of the heart proceed evil thoughts, murders, adulteries, fornications, thefts, lies and blasphemies. These are the things that defile a man, but to eat with unwashed hands does not defile a man."*

The Gospel of Jesus the Christ

Peter Recognizes Jesus As The Christ

Jesus and his disciples left and went into the coasts of Caesarea Philippi. Jesus asked his disciples, *"Who do the people say that I am?"* The disciples said, "Some say that you are John the Baptist, some say that you are Elijah, and others say that you are Jeremiah or one of the prophets." Jesus asked them, *"Who do you say that I am?"* Peter answered and said, "You are the Christ, the Son of the living God."

Jesus said to him, *"Blessed are you, Simon Peter, for this was not revealed to you by men, but by God. I say to you that you are Peter and upon this rock I will build my church, and the gates of hades will not prevail against it. And I will give to you the keys to the kingdom of heaven. Whatever you bind on earth will be bound in heaven, and whatever you loose on earth will be loosed in heaven."* Then Jesus told his disciples to tell no one that he was the Christ until after he had risen from the dead.

The Gospel of Jesus the Christ

John The Baptist Is Beheaded

At that time the tetrarch, Herod Antipas, heard of the fame of Jesus. He said to his servants, "This is John the Baptist, who has risen from the dead. That is how these mighty works are being done."

Herod had arrested John and had him thrown into prison for the sake of Herodias, his brother Phillip's wife. John had said to him, "It is not lawful for you to have her."

When Herod's birthday had arrived, the daughter of Herodias danced before Herod and the guests, and pleased Herod. Then Herod promised with an oath to give her whatever she desired. She said, "Give me the head of John the Baptist on a platter."

The king was very sorry. Nevertheless, for the oath's sake and because of the dinner guests, he commanded that it be given to her. Then he had John beheaded in the prison and his head was brought to the damsel on a platter, and she gave it to her mother.

The Gospel of Jesus the Christ

Jesus Foretells Of His Death

From that time on Jesus began to tell his disciples how he must go into Jerusalem and suffer many things at the hands of the chief priests and Pharisees. And he told them how he was to be killed and raised again on the third day. Then Peter said, "Lord, this will not happen to you!"

Jesus turned to Peter and said, *"Get behind me! You are a stumbling block to me, for you have in mind the things of men and not of God.*

If anyone comes after me, let him deny himself and take up his cross and follow me. Whoever saves his own life will lose it, and whoever loses his own life for my sake will find it.

What does it profit a man to gain the whole world and lose his own soul? What shall someone give in exchange for his soul?

The Son of Man will come in the glory of his Father with his angels and will reward every person according to their deeds. Verily, I say to you that there will be some who are standing here that will not taste of death until they see the Son of Man coming in his kingdom."

The Gospel of Jesus the Christ

The Transfiguration Of Jesus

After six days Jesus took Peter, James and John his brother, up to a high mountain. Jesus was transfigured in front of them. His face shone as the sun and his clothes were as white as the light. There in front of them appeared Moses and Elijah talking with Jesus. Peter said to Jesus, "Master, it is good that we are here. If you wish, we will build three shelters; one for you, one for Moses and one for Elijah."

While Peter was speaking, a bright cloud overshadowed them and a voice came from heaven saying, "This is my beloved Son, in whom I am well pleased. Listen to him!" When the disciples heard this they fell on their faces and were very afraid. Jesus came and touched them and said, *"Get up, and do not be afraid."* When they lifted up their eyes they saw no one, except Jesus.

As they came down the mountain Jesus instructed them, saying, *"Don't tell anyone about this vision until the Son of Man has risen from the dead."*

His disciples asked him, "Why do the priests

say that Elijah must come first?" Jesus answered them, *"Elijah does come first and restores all things. I tell you the truth when I say that Elijah has already come, and they did not recognize him. They made him suffer many things and killed him. So also will the Son of Man be made to suffer by them."* Then the disciples understood that he was speaking about John the Baptist.

The Power Of Faith

When they returned to the multitude a man came to Jesus and said, "Lord, please have mercy on my son. He is insane and sometimes he falls into the fire, and sometimes he falls into the water. I brought him to your disciples, but they could not cure him." Jesus said, *"O faithless and perverse generation, how long shall I suffer you? Bring the boy here to me."* Then Jesus rebuked the demon and the spirit departed out of him, and the child was healed from that very hour.

Afterward the disciples came to Jesus saying, "Why couldn't we cure him?" Jesus said to them, *"It is because of your unbelief. Verily I say to you that if you have faith as a grain of mustard seed, then you can say to a mountain 'throw yourself into the sea' and it will be done. If you believe and have no doubts in your heart, then nothing would be impossible for you. However, this kind of faith only comes through prayer and fasting."*

As they were leaving, two blind men sitting by the road called out to Jesus, "Lord, son of David, have mercy on us!"

Jesus called them to him and asked them, *"What would you like me to do for you?"* They said, "Lord, please open our eyes."

Jesus asked them, *"Do you believe that I am able to do this?"* They answered, "Yes, Lord." Then Jesus touched their eyes saying, *"According to your faith, it is done to you."* Their eyes were opened and Jesus said to them, *"Do not tell anyone about this."* But after they left, they spread his fame all around that country.

After Jesus and his disciples arrived in Capernaum the collectors of the two-drachma tax said to Peter, "Does your Master pay the temple tax?" Peter answered, "Yes."

Then Peter went into the house where Jesus was staying and Jesus said to him, *"What do you think, Peter? From whom do the kings of the earth* collect duty and taxes, from their own children or from strangers?" Peter answered, "From strangers."

Jesus said, "Then their children are exempt. Nevertheless, so that we do not offend them, go to the lake and throw out a fishing line. Take the first fish that you catch, open its mouth, and in it you will find a four-drachma coin. Go and give it to the collectors for my tax and yours."

Who Is Greatest In The Kingdom Of Heaven

The disciples came to Jesus, saying, "Who is the greatest in the kingdom of heaven?" Jesus called a little child to him and set him in the middle of them and said, "Verily I say to you, unless you are converted and become as little children you will not enter into the kingdom of heaven.

Whoever, therefore, humbles himself like this little child is the greatest in the kingdom of heaven. And whoever receives such a little child in my name receives me, but whoever causes one of these little ones who believe in me to sin, it would be better for him that a millstone is hung around his neck and he drown in the depth of the sea.

Be careful that you do not harm one of these little

ones. I say to you that in heaven their angels always see the face of God!

Woe to this world because of sin! It is necessary for evil to exist, but woe to the one from whom the evil comes!

Therefore, if your hand or your foot causes you to sin, then cut them off and throw them away. It is better to enter heaven with only one hand or one foot than to be thrown into hell with both hands or both feet.

And if your eye causes you to sin, then pluck it out and throw it away! It is better to enter into heaven with one eye than to be thrown into hell with both eyes."

How Often Someone Should Forgive

Peter came to Jesus and said, "Master, how often should I forgive someone who sins against me? Seven times?" Jesus said, "No, not seven times, but seventy times seven times.

Therefore, the kingdom of heaven is like a king who went to settle accounts with his servants. When he had begun the settlement process a subject who owed him ten thousand talents came to him. Since the man didn't have the money to repay him, the king ordered

that he and his wife and children, along with everything they owned, to be sold in order to repay him.

The man fell to his knees and begged the king
saying, 'Lord, please have patience with me, and I will
repay all that I owe to you.' The king was moved with
compassion and let the man go and forgave him the
debt.

That same man went out and found a fellow servant who owed him a hundred pennies. He laid his
hands on him and grabbed him by the throat, saying,
'Pay to me what you owe!'

His fellow servant fell to his knees and begged him,
saying, 'Please have patience with me, and I will pay
to you all that I owe.' The man would not give him
any more time to repay the debt, but instead had
him thrown into prison.

When his fellow servants saw what he had done,
they went to the king and told him everything they had
seen. Then the king called the man to him and said,
'You wicked servant! I forgave you all that you
owed because you begged me. Why didn't you have
compassion on your fellow servant, as I had pity on
you?'

The king was furious and he delivered the man to
the jailors to be tortured until he could pay back the

entire debt. So likewise, will God do to you, if you do not forgive from your hearts all those who trespass against you.

Moreover, if your brother or sister transgresses against you, you should go and tell him his fault between you and him alone. If he hears you, then you have gained back your brother or sister. I say to you that if two of you agree on earth that something shall be done in my name, then it shall be done for you by my Father in heaven. For wherever two or more of you are gathered together in my name, there I will be also."

Jesus Speaks About Divorce

After Jesus had finished saying these things he departed from Galilee and went into the coasts of Judea. Great multitudes followed him and he healed their sick.

The Pharisees also came to Jesus, trying to trap him, saying, "Is it lawful for a man to divorce his wife for any reason?" Jesus answered them, *"Haven't you read that in the beginning 'the Creator made them male and female, and for this reason a man shall leave his family and shall cleave to his wife, and they will no longer be two, but shall be one flesh'? They are no longer two, but one. Therefore, what God has put together let no one separate."*

They asked him, "Why did Moses command that a man give his wife a certificate of divorcement and send her away?"

Jesus said, *"It is because your hearts were hard that Moses commanded this, but in the beginning it was not so. Furthermore, I say to you that any man who divorces his wife, except for the act of marital unfaithfulness, and marries another woman commits adultery. And whoever marries the divorced woman commits adultery. And if a woman divorces her husband, except for the act of adultery, and marries another man, then she commits adultery."* The disciples said to Jesus, "If this is the case between a husband and wife, then it is better not to marry." Jesus said, *"Not everyone can receive this, but only those to whom it has been given by God. There are some who were born as eunuchs from their mother's womb and there are some who were made into eunuchs by others, and there are some who have made themselves eunuchs for the sake of the Kingdom of God. Those who are able to receive this let them receive it."*

The Gospel of Jesus the Christ

The Reward Of Heaven

As Jesus was leaving from there a man came to him and said, "Good Master, what good thing must I do in order to obtain eternal life?"

Jesus answered him, *"Why do you call me 'good'? There is only One who is 'good' and that One is God. But if you want to enter into eternal life then keep the commandments."*

He said, "Which ones?" Jesus replied, *"Do not murder, do not steal, do not lie, do not commit adultery, honor your mother and father, and love your neighbor as yourself."* The young man said to Jesus, "All of these commandments I have kept since childhood. What more do I lack?"
Jesus said to him, *"If you want to be perfect then go and sell all that you own and give the money to the poor, and you will have treasure in heaven. Then come and follow me."*

When the young man heard this he went away very sad, because he had great wealth and many possessions. Jesus said to his disciples, *"Verily, I say to you that a rich person will rarely enter into the kingdom of heaven. It is easier for a camel to go through the eye of the needle than for a rich person* to enter into the Kingdom of God."

The disciples said, "Who then can be saved?" Jesus said, *"With men this would be impossible, but with God all things are possible."*

Then Peter said, "Look, we have given up everything and followed you! What will be our reward?"

Jesus said, *"I say to you that you who have followed me, in the next life, at the regeneration of all things, when the Son of Man sits on his throne of glory, you also will sit upon twelve thrones, judging the twelve tribes of Israel.*

Everyone who has given up houses, or brothers, or sisters, or father, or mother, or wife, or children, or lands for my sake will receive a hundred-fold and will inherit everlasting life. But many that are first will be last, and the last will be first."

The Parable Of The Workers In The Vineyard

Then Jesus taught another parable, saying, *"The kingdom of heaven is like a householder who went out early in the morning to hire laborers to work in his vineyard. He agreed to pay each laborer a dollar a day for their compensation. Then he sent them into* his vineyard to work.

The householder went out around the third hour and saw others standing idle in the marketplace. He said to them, 'You also go to my vineyard, and I will pay you whatever is right.' And they went to work in the vineyard.

He went out around the sixth and ninth hour and likewise found more workers for his vineyard. About the eleventh hour the householder went out and found others standing idle and he asked them, 'Why do you stand idle here all day long?' They answered, 'It is because no one has hired us.' The householder said, 'Go to my vineyard and work, and I will pay you whatever is right.'

When evening came the master of the vineyard said to his steward, 'Call the laborers and give them their pay, beginning with the last ones hired.'

When those that were hired around the eleventh hour came to receive their pay, they each were given one dollar. Likewise, those called at the ninth and sixth hours were each given one dollar. When those who were hired at the first hour came to receive their pay, they also were given one dollar.

The ones that had been hired at the first hour began to complain to the owner of the vineyard saying,

'The laborers who were called last have only worked one hour and you have made them equal to those of us who have endured the burden and the heat of the day.'

The householder answered one of them and said, 'Friend, I do you no wrong. Didn't you agree to work for one dollar? Take your pay and go your way. Isn't it lawful that I can do as I wish with that which is mine? Are you angry because I am generous?'

So the last will be first, and the first will be last. Many are called, but few are chosen."

The Parable Of The Wedding Banquet

Jesus told another parable saying, "The kingdom of heaven is like a certain king who arranged a marriage for his son. He sent his servants to call those who had been invited to the wedding, but they would not come. He sent other servants to tell those who were invited, 'Look, the table is ready! The oxen and fattened cattle have been prepared and everything is ready. Come to the wedding banquet!' But they made light of it and went their separate ways, one to his farm and another to his merchandise. The remainder took the king's servants, mistreated and killed them.

When the king heard about this he became enraged. He sent out his armies to destroy those murderers and burn down their cities. Then he said to the rest of his servants, 'The wedding is ready, but those who were invited were not worthy. Go to the highways and streets and invite everyone that you can find to come to the wedding.'

So the servants went out and found many people, both good and bad, to come to the wedding and the wedding was furnished with guests.

When the king came in to see the guests, he saw a man who was not wearing wedding clothes. The king said to the man, 'Friend, how did you get in here without wearing wedding clothes?' The man was speechless. Then the king said to his servants, 'Bind him hand and foot and throw him outside, into the outer darkness. Many are called, but few are chosen.' "

Jesus Again Predicts His Death

As they were traveling to Jerusalem, Jesus took the twelve disciples apart from the crowd and said to them, "We will go to Jerusalem and the Son of Man will be betrayed, and will be brought up before the chief priests and elders of the law and they will condemn him to death. *They will deliver him to the Gentiles to mock and scourge. They will crucify him and on the third day after his death he will be raised from the dead.*"

The mother of Zebedee's sons came to Jesus and said, "Lord, grant that my sons may sit, one at your right hand and the other at your left hand, in your kingdom."

Jesus said to her, "*You do not understand what you are asking of me.*" He asked the two brothers, "*Are you able to drink of the cup that I will drink and to be baptized with the baptism that I am baptized with?*" They answered, "Yes, we are able." Jesus said to them, "*You, indeed, will drink from my cup and be baptized with the Holy Spirit, but to sit on my right hand and on my left is not mine to give. It will be given to those for whom it was prepared by God.*"

When the other ten disciples heard this they became angry with the two brothers. Jesus said, "*You know that the kings and princes of the Gentiles exercise authority over the people under them, but it will not be so among you.*

Whoever will be great among you, let him be your minister. And whoever will be the chief among you, let him be your servant. Even the Son of Man came not to be ministered to but to minister, and to give his life as a ransom for many."

Jesus Stays At Zacharias' House

A very rich publican named Zacharias found out that Jesus was among them. Wanting to see Jesus, but because he was small in stature and could not see above the crowd, Zacharias climbed up into a sycamore tree.

When Jesus came by that place he looked up and saw him in the tree. Then Jesus said to him, "Zacharias, come down from the tree, because today I need to stay at your house." Zacharias came down immediately, and joyfully went to Jesus.

When those who were in the crowd saw this they murmured among themselves, saying, "Jesus has gone to be a guest in the house of a sinner." Zacharias stood and said to Jesus, "Look! I will give half of everything I own to the poor, and if I have taken anything away from anyone by deceit I will repay it back to him fourfold."

Jesus said to him, *"Today salvation has come to this house, for you are also a son of Abraham. The Son* of Man has come to save those who are lost. *What do you think? If a man has a hundred sheep and one of them wanders off, does he leave the ninety-nine to go into the mountain and find the one that has wandered off? And if he finds it, he rejoices more over that sheep than the ninety-nine that did not wander off. I say to you that there is more joy in heaven over one sinner that repents than ninety-nine just persons that need no repentance. And what woman, having ten pieces of silver, if she loses one piece, does not light a candle and sweep the house, looking diligently until she finds it? And when she finds it she calls her friends and neighbors together, saying, 'Rejoice with me, for I have found the piece which I had lost.'*

I say to you that there is joy in the presence of the angels of God over one sinner who repents."

Then Jesus spoke a parable saying, *"Two men went into the temple to pray; one was a Pharisee and the other was a publican.*

The Pharisee stood and prayed thus: 'God, I thank you that I am not like other men: extortionists, unjust, adulterers, or even as this publican. I fast twice in the week and I give tithes of all that I possess.'

The publican, standing far away, would not even lift up his eyes to heaven. He smote his breast saying,

'God, be merciful to me a sinner.'

I tell you that the publican went back to his house justified rather than the Pharisee. Everyone that exalts himself will be humbled, and everyone that humbles himself will be exalted."

The Parable Of The Prodigal Son

Jesus told another parable, saying, "A certain man had two sons. The younger son said to his father, 'Father, give me my portion of the inheritance now.' The father divided his living between them and a few days later the younger son gathered together everything he owned and left. He journeyed into a far country and there he squandered his inheritance on riotous living.

When the younger son had spent all that he had there arose a terrible famine throughout the land, and he began to be in need. Then he went and worked for a citizen in that country, feeding swine. And he filled his belly with the husks that the swine ate.

When he came to himself he said, 'How many hired servants of my father's have enough bread to spare, as I starve to death! I will go to my father and say to him, "Father, I have sinned against heaven and against you. I am no longer worthy to be called your son. Make me as one of your hired servants." '

Then he got up and went to his father's house. While he was still a distance away, his father saw him approaching and he had compassion on his son. The father ran to him and fell on his neck, and kissed him.

The son said, 'Father, I have sinned against heaven and against you. I am no longer worthy to be called your son. Make me as one of your hired servants.'

The father said to his servants, 'Bring the best robe and put it on him. Put a ring on his finger and shoes on his feet. And bring the fattened calf, let us eat and be merry. My son was dead, and now he is alive again. He was lost, but now is found.' Then they began to eat and be merry.

When the elder son came from the field he heard the music and saw the dancing. He called one of the servants over to him and asked what these things meant. The servant told him, 'Your brother has come home, and your father has killed the fattened calf because he has received him safe and sound.'

The elder son became angry and refused to go in, so his father came out to him and pleaded with him. He said to his father, 'Look! All of these years I have been faithful and served you. Yet, you never gave a fattened calf to me, so that I might make merry with *my friends. But as soon as your other son returned after devouring your living with harlots, you have given him the fattened calf.'*

The father replied, 'Son, you are forever with me, and all that I have is also yours. It is good that we should make merry and be glad, for your brother was dead, and is alive again. He was lost, but now is found.'

Likewise, it is the will of God that no one should be lost."

The Parable Of The Unjust Steward

Then Jesus spoke another parable, saying, *"There was a certain rich man who had a steward. The rich man had accused his steward of wasting his goods. He called the steward to him and said, 'How is it that I hear that you have wasted my goods? Give an account of your stewardship, for you may no longer be my steward.' The steward said within himself, 'What will I do if my lord takes away my stewardship? I cannot dig, and I am too ashamed to beg. I know what I will do, so that when I am put out of the stewardship I may be welcomed into their houses.' So he called every one of his lord's debtors to him and he asked the*

*first, 'How much do you owe to my lord?' The debtor
replied, 'A hundred measures of oil.' The steward said
to him, 'Take your bill and sit down quickly, and write
it out for fifty.' Then he asked another, 'How much do
you owe?' And he said, 'A hundred measures of wheat.'
The steward said to him, 'Take your bill and write
fourscore.'*

*Then the lord commended the unjust steward
because he had done wisely, for the children of this
world are in their generation wiser than the children
of light. Therefore, make friends of the mammon of un-
righteousness so that, if you fail, they may receive you
into everlasting habitations. He that is faithful in that
which is least will be faithful also in much, and he
that is unjust in the least is also unjust in much.*

*If you have not been faithful with the unrighteous
mammon, then who will commit to your trust the true
riches? And if you have not been faithful with that
which belongs to another, then who will trust you
with that which is your own?"*

The Pharisees, who were covetous, heard
these things and derided Jesus. Jesus said to
them, "*You justify yourselves before men, but God
knows your hearts. That which is highly esteemed
among men is an abomination in the sight of God.*"

The Gospel of Jesus the Christ

The Parable Of The Beggar And The Rich Man

Jesus told another parable, saying, *"There was a certain rich man who was clothed in purple and fine linen, and he lived extravagantly every day. And there was a certain beggar named Lazarus who lay at the rich man's gate, full of sores. Lazarus begged to be fed from the crumbs that fell from the rich man's table, and the dogs came and licked his sores.*

And it came to pass that the beggar died and was carried by the angels into Abraham's bosom. The rich man also died and was buried. And in hell he lifted up his eyes, being in torment, and he saw Abraham afar off, with Lazarus in his bosom. He cried out, 'Father Abraham, have mercy on me! Send Lazarus so that he may dip the tip of his finger in water and cool my tongue, for I am tormented in this flame.'

Abraham said, 'Son, remember that in your lifetime you had many riches and received good things. Likewise, Lazarus received bad things. But now he is comforted, and you are tormented. Besides all this, there is a great fixed gulf between us, so that no one can pass from here to there, nor can anyone pass from there to here.'

Then the rich man said, 'I pray to you, father

Abraham, to send Lazarus to my father's house, so that he may warn my brothers about this place of torment.' Abraham said to him, 'They have Moses and the prophets, let them hear them.' The rich man said, 'No, father Abraham, but if one went to them from the dead, then they would repent.' Abraham said, 'If they will not hear Moses and the prophets, then neither will they be persuaded even though one rose from the dead.' "

When the Pharisees demanded to know when the kingdom of heaven would come Jesus said, *"The kingdom of heaven does not come through observation. Neither shall anyone say, 'Look here!' or 'Look there!' because the kingdom of heaven is within you."*

Jesus Goes To Jerusalem

When they came to Bethphage, to the Mount of Olives, Jesus sent out two of his disciples saying to them, *"Go into the village and you will find a donkey tied, and a colt with her. Bring them here to me, and if anyone questions you, say, 'The Lord needs them.' "*

This was done so that the prophecy would be

fulfilled: "Tell the daughter of Zion that her King comes to her meek and sitting on a donkey, bringing a colt, the foal of a donkey."

The disciples went and did as Jesus had commanded. A great multitude went ahead of Jesus into Jerusalem crying out, "Hosanna to the son of David! Blessed is the One that comes in the name of God! Hosanna in the highest!"

When Jesus had come into Jerusalem everyone in the city was moved, saying, "Who is this?" The crowd answered, "This is Jesus, the prophet from Nazareth in Galilee."

When Jesus came to the temple he saw the rich men putting their gifts into the treasury. And he also saw a certain poor widow putting two cents into the treasury. Jesus said, "*I tell you the truth, that this poor widow has put in more than all of the others. For the others have made their offerings to God out of the abundance of their possessions, but this poor widow has given all that she has.*"

Jesus went into the temple and threw out everyone who was buying and selling merchandise. He overturned the tables of the moneychangers and the seats of the merchants. Jesus said to them, "*It is written, 'My house shall be called a house of prayer' but you have made it into a den of thieves!"*

Then the blind and the lame came to Jesus in the temple, and he healed them all.

When the chief priests and the elders of the law saw all the wonderful miracles that Jesus performed and all the children crying in the temple, saying, "Hosanna to the son of David!" they were very displeased. They said to Jesus, "By what authority do you do these things?"

Jesus said to them, *"I will answer your question about with what authority I do these things if you will answer my question, 'Was the baptism of John by heaven or by men?' "*

They reasoned among themselves, saying, "If we say, 'by heaven' then he will say to us, 'Why didn't you believe him?' but if we say, 'by men' then the crowd will be angry because they believe John was a prophet." They answered Jesus and said, "We cannot tell."

Jesus said to them, *"Then neither can I tell you by what authority I do these things.*

What do you think? A certain man had two sons. He went to the first son and said, 'Son, go work today in my vineyard.' The first son answered and said, 'I

271

will not' but afterward he repented and went. Then the man went to his second son and said likewise, 'Go and work today in my vineyard.' The second son said 'I will go, sir' but he did not go. Which of the two did the will of his father?"

They said to him, "The first." Then Jesus said to them, "*I say to you that the publicans and prostitutes will go into the Kingdom of God before you.*

For John came to you in righteousness and you did not believe him, but the publicans and prostitutes believed him. And you did not repent afterwards, so that you could believe him.

Hear another parable. There was a certain householder who planted a vineyard and hedged around it. He dug a winepress in it and built a tower. Then he lent it out to farmers and went into a far country. When the time for the harvesting of the fruit drew near, he sent his servants to collect the fruit from the farmers.

The farmers took his servants, beat one, killed one and stoned another. Again, he sent other servants and the farmers treated those servants the same as the first. Last of all he sent his own son, saying, 'They will respect my own son.'

The Gospel of Jesus the Christ

When the farmers saw the son they said among themselves, 'This is the heir. Come, let us kill him and then we can take possession of his inheritance.' They caught him, took him out of the vineyard and killed him. When the lord of the vineyard comes back, what will he do to those men?"

The chief priests said to Jesus, "He will miserably destroy those evil men, and he will lend out his vineyard to other farmers who will render to him the fruits in their seasons."

Jesus said to them, *"Have you never read in the scriptures, 'The stone which the builders rejected becomes the cornerstone of the building. This is the Lord's doing and it is marvelous in his eyes'?*

Therefore, I say to you that the Kingdom of God will be taken from you and given to a nation that will produce fruit for the kingdom. Whoever falls on this stone will be broken, but on whomever this stone falls, it will grind him to powder."

When the chief priests and Pharisees heard this, they perceived Jesus was speaking about them. When they sought to lay hands on him they feared the crowds because they believed Jesus was a prophet.

Who Should Pay Taxes To Caesar

The Pharisees went and gathered together
to see how they might entangle Jesus in his teachings. They sent to him disciples of the Herodians
who said to Jesus, "Master, we know that you are
a man of truth and that you do not care about
the opinions of other men, and we know that
you do not care about the positions of other
men. Tell us then, is it right to pay taxes to
Caesar?"

Jesus answered them, *"Why do you tempt me,
you hypocrites? Show me the tax money."* They
brought him a penny. Jesus said to them,
"Whose image is on the inscription?" They said to
him, "Caesar's." Jesus replied, *"Give to Caesar
what is Caesar's and give to God what is God's."*
When they heard these words they marveled
and left him and went their way.

Jesus Is Invited To The Chief Pharisee's House

And it came to pass; Jesus was invited to the
chief Pharisee's house to eat bread. Jesus noticed
how the other guests who were invited chose out

the chief rooms and he said to them, *"When you are invited to dinner do not sit down in the highest room, lest a more honorable person than yourself is invited and the host says to you, 'Give your seat to this man.' Then you will have to move to a lower room.*

Instead, when you are invited, go and sit in the lowest room. Then the host may say to you, 'Friend, go up higher,' and you will be respected by the other guests.

Whoever exalts himself will be humbled, and whoever humbles himself will be exalted."

Then Jesus said to the Pharisee who had invited him, *"When you make a dinner, don't call your friends, or your family or your rich neighbors to the feast. They may invite you in return, and in this way they will compensate you.*

Instead, when you make a dinner, invite the poor, the maimed, the lame and the blind. They will not be able to compensate you, and you will receive your reward at the resurrection of the just."

Jesus Defends The Woman Accused Of Adultery

Early in the morning Jesus went again to the temple and the people came to him, and he taught them many things. The scribes and Pharisees brought a woman who had been charged with adultery to Jesus. They said to him, "Master, this woman here has committed adultery. She was caught in the very act! Moses commanded that she be stoned to death, but what do you say?"

Jesus stooped down and wrote on the ground with his finger, as though he didn't hear them. When they continued asking him, he got up and said to them, *"Whoever is without sin among you, let him throw the first stone at her."* Then again he stooped down and began writing on the ground.

The people, by their own conscious, left one by one, and Jesus was left alone with the woman. When Jesus got up he saw no one except the woman and he said to her, *"Woman, where are your accusers? Has any man condemned you?"* She said, "No man, Lord." Then Jesus said to her, *"Neither do I condemn you. Go in peace, and sin no more."*

The Gospel of Jesus the Christ

Jesus Raises Lazarus From The Dead

Lazarus of Bethany, who was a friend of Jesus and the brother of Martha and Mary, lay very ill. His sisters went to Jesus and said, "Lord, your friend whom you love is very sick."

Jesus said to them, *"This sickness is for the glory of God, so that the Son of God may be glorified."* When Jesus heard about Lazarus he stayed where he was another two days and then he said to his disciples, *"Let us return to Judea again."*

The disciples said to him, "Master, lately the Pharisees have sought to stone you. Why would you return there again?"

Jesus answered, *"Are there not twelve hours in a day? If anyone walks in the daytime he will not stumble, because he has the light of the world to see. But if someone walks at night he stumbles because there is no light to see. Our friend Lazarus is sleeping. I must go and wake him."*

The disciples said, "Lord, if Lazarus is sleeping then he will recover." Jesus said to them plainly, *"Lazarus is dead. I am glad for your sakes that I was not there, because now you will believe. Nevertheless, let us go to him."*

When Jesus came to Bethany he found out that Lazarus had had been dead for four days. Martha went out to meet Jesus and said to him, "Lord, if you had been here my brother would not have died."

Jesus said to her, *"Your brother will rise again."* Martha said, "I know he will rise again at the resurrection on the last day."

Jesus said to her, *"I am the the resurrection and the life. The one who believes in me, even though he is like the dead, will live again. And whoever lives and believes in me will never die. Do you believe this?"*

Martha said, "Yes, Lord, I believe that you are the Christ, the Son of God." Then she went and called her sister, Mary, saying, "The Master has come." As soon as Mary heard this she got up quickly and went out to meet Jesus. The Jews who were with her in the house got up and followed her.

When Mary arrived where Jesus was she fell down at his feet and said to him, "Lord, if you had been here my brother would not have died."

Jesus said, *"Where have you laid him?"* They said to him, "Lord, come and see." Jesus wept. The Jews said, "Look how he loved him!" And some of them said, "Could not this man, who opened the eyes of the blind, have prevented this man from dying?"

Jesus came to the grave. It was a cave, and a stone was placed in front of the entrance. Jesus said, *"Take away the stone."*

Martha said to him, "Lord, by this time he must stink terribly, for he has been in the grave four days!" Jesus said, *"Didn't I say that if you believe, you would see the glory of God?"*

They took away the stone from the entrance to the cave. Jesus lifted up his eyes to heaven and said, *"God, I thank you for hearing me, and I know that you always hear me. I said this for the benefit of the people standing here, so that they will believe that you have sent me."*

After saying this Jesus cried out with a loud voice, *"Lazarus, come out!"* Then Lazarus walked out of the cave, bound hand and foot with grave clothes and his face was bound with a cloth. Jesus said to the people standing by, *"Unbind him and let him go."*

Many of the people who saw these things believed on Jesus, but some of them went to the Pharisees and told them what Jesus had done.

The Gospel of Jesus the Christ

Jesus Again Teaches In The Temple

Early in the morning Jesus went to the Mount of Olives and went again into the temple. All the people came to him and he taught them saying, *"I am the light of the world. The one who follows me shall not walk in darkness, but shall have the light of life.*

And if anyone hears my words and does not believe, I will not judge him. I did not come to judge the world, but to save it. The one who rejects me and does not believe my words has one that judges him; the Word that I have spoken, the same will judge him on the last day.

I have not spoken of myself, but of God that sent me. He gave me a commandment of what to speak. And I know that his commandment is eternal life. Whatever I speak, therefore, is coming from God."

The Pharisees said to him, "You bare record of yourself. Therefore your record is not true." Jesus said to them, *"Though I bare record of myself, my record is true. I know where I came from and where I am going, but you cannot tell where I came from or where I go. You judge after things of the flesh, and I judge no one. It is also written in your law that the testimony of two men is true. I am one that bears witness of myself, and my Father that sent me bears witness of me."*

They asked Jesus, "Where is your Father?" Jesus answered, *"You do not know me or my Father. If you had known me you would have known my Father also."*

Jesus Is The Good Shepherd

Then Jesus spoke a parable saying, *"Verily, verily, I say to you that the one who enters not by the door into the flock, but climbs in some other way; the same is a thief and a robber. But the one who enters in by the door is the shepherd of the flock.*

The portal opens for him and his sheep hear his voice. He calls his own sheep by name and leads them out.

And when he sends forth his own sheep, he goes before them and the sheep follow him, for they know his voice. They will not follow a stranger but instead will flee from him, because they know not the voice of strangers."

Jesus spoke this parable to them, but they did not understand what he said. Jesus spoke to them again, saying, "Verily, verily, I say to you that I am the door of the sheep. All who ever came before me are thieves and robbers, and my sheep did not hear them.

I am the door. If anyone enters in through me he will be saved, and he shall go in and out and find pasture.

The thief comes to steal, and to kill and destroy. I have come so that people might have life, and have it more abundantly.

I am the good shepherd. The good shepherd gives his life for his sheep. I know my sheep and my sheep know me. And other sheep I have, which are not of this fold; those also I must bring. And they shall hear my voice and there shall be one fold, and one shepherd.

Therefore, God loves me because I lay down my life for my sheep. No one takes it from me, but I lay it down myself. I have the power to lay it down and I have the power to take it again; this God has revealed unto me. I go my way, and you shall look for me and die in your sins, for where I am going, you cannot come."

The Pharisees said, "Will he kill himself? What does he mean when he says, 'where I am going, you cannot come?'" Jesus said to them,

"You are from beneath, I am from above. You are of this world, I am not of this world. I say, therefore, that you will die in your sins if you do not believe that I am the Christ."

There was a division among the people because of these sayings. Many of the people said, "He has a devil and is crazy! Why do you listen to him?" Others said, "These are not the words of someone who has a devil. Can a devil open the eyes of the blind?"

Jesus Compares Himself With God

In Jerusalem, at the feast of the dedication, Jesus walked in the temple on Solomon's porch. The Pharisees came to him and said, "How long will you make us doubt? If you are the Messiah, then tell us plainly." Jesus said to them, *"I told you and you did not believe me. The works that I do by my Father's authority bear witness of me. You do not believe because you are not my sheep. As I already said to you, 'My sheep recognize me and I know them, and they follow me.' And I give to them eternal life, and they shall never perish. Neither shall any man pluck them out of my hand. My Father, which has given* them to me, is greater than all. No man is able to pluck them out of my Father's hand. I and my Father are One."

Then the Pharisees gathered up stones to stone him. Jesus asked them, "I have showed you many good works from my Father, for which of those works do you stone me?" The Pharisees answered him, "We do not stone you for a good work, but for blasphemy. And because you, being a man, make yourself God." Jesus said, "Is it not written in your law concerning the prophets: 'I said, you are gods'? If he called those to whom the Word of God was given 'gods' then the scripture cannot be broken. Do you say of Him whom God has sanctified, 'you blaspheme' because I said, 'I am the Son of God'? If I do not do the works of my Father, then don't believe me. But if I do, even if you do not believe me, then believe the works. Then you will know that my Father is in me, and I am in my Father."

Jesus Talks About Abraham's Seed

As Jesus spoke these words many people believed on him. Jesus said to those people who believed on him, "If you continue in my Word, then you are my disciples indeed. And you will know the Truth, and the Truth will make you free."

The Pharisees said to him, "We are Abraham's seed and were never in bondage to any man. How can you say that we will be made free?" Jesus said to them, "Verily, I say to you that whoever commits sin is the servant of sin. The servant does not abide in the house forever, but the Son abides in the house forever. If the Son, therefore, shall make you free, then you shall be free indeed.

I know that you are Abraham's seed, but you seek to kill me because my Words have no place in you. I speak that which I have seen with my Father, and you do that which you have seen with your father."

They said to him, "Abraham is our father." Jesus said, "If you were Abraham's children then you would do the works of Abraham. You seek to kill me, a man who has told you the truth, which I have heard from God. Abraham did not do this. You do the deeds of your father."

Then they said to him, "We are not born of fornication; we have one Father, which is God." Jesus said to them, "If God were your Father then you would love me, because I came from God. I did not come of my own will, but God sent me. Why can't you understand my message? It is because you cannot hear my Word. You are of your father, the devil, and you do the desires of your father. He was a murderer from the beginning, and he does not abide in the Truth because there is no truth in him. When he speaks a lie, he speaks of his own because he is a liar and the father of lies. I tell you the Truth and you do not believe me. And if I tell you the Truth, why don't you believe me? Those that are of God hear God's Words. You do not hear them because you are not of God."

The Pharisees said to Jesus, "Didn't we say that you are crazy and that you have a devil?" Jesus answered, "I do not have a devil. I honor my Father, and you dishonor me. Verily, verily, I say to you that whoever keeps my teachings will never see death."

Then the Pharisees said to him, "Now we know that you have a devil. Abraham and the prophets are dead and you say, 'Whoever keeps my teachings will never see death.' Are you greater than our father, Abraham, which is dead? And are you greater than the prophets, which are dead? Who do you think you are?"

Jesus answered, "If I honor myself, then my honor means nothing. My Father, whom you say is your God, *honors me. Yet you have never known him, but I know him. And if I were to say that I do not know Him, then I would be a liar like you. But I do know Him, and I keep his Word. Your father Abraham rejoiced to see my day, and he saw it and was glad."*

Some of the Pharisees said to him, "You are not even fifty years old, and you have seen Abraham?" Jesus said to them, *"Verily, verily, I say to you that before Abraham was, I am."*

Then they again picked up stones to throw at Jesus, but Jesus hid himself and left the temple, passing through the middle of them.

Jesus Makes The Blind Man See

As Jesus passed by, he saw a man who had been blind since birth. His disciples asked, "Master, who sinned, this man or his parents, so that he was born blind?" Jesus answered, *"Neither this man or his parents has sinned, so that he was born blind. It is so that the miracles of God can be shown in him. I must work the works of the One who has sent me while there is daylight. Soon the night will come, and no man can work. As long as I am in the world, I am the light of the world."*

The Gospel of Jesus the Christ

After he had spoken, Jesus spit on the ground and made clay from the spittle. He anointed the eyes of the blind man with the clay and he said to him, *"Go and wash in the pool of Siloam."* The blind man went his way and washed, and was able to see.

The neighbors, who had known him before when he was blind, said, "Isn't he the one who sat and begged?" Some said, "that is him", and others said, "it looks like him" and then the man said, "It is me." Then they asked him, "How were your eyes opened?" He answered, "A man that is called Jesus made clay, and he rubbed my eyes with the clay and told me to go wash in the pool of Siloam. I went and washed, and I received my sight." They asked him, "Where is he?" The man answered, "I do not know."

Then they brought the former blind man to the Pharisees. And it was the Sabbath day when Jesus had made the clay and opened the man's eyes. The Pharisees asked him again how he had received his sight. He said to them, "He put clay upon my eyes, and I washed and now I can see." Therefore some of the Pharisees said, "This man is not of God, because he does not observe the

Sabbath day." Others said, "How can a man that is a sinner do such miracles?" And they were divided over Jesus. They asked the former blind man, "What do you have to say about the man who opened your eyes?" The man said, "He is a prophet."

Some of the Pharisees did not believe that the man had been born blind, so they called together the parents of the man who had received his sight. They asked his parents, "Is this your son, who you say was born blind? How is it that he now sees?" His parents answered, "We know that this is our son and that he was born blind, but we do not know by who or by what means he has received his sight. Ask him yourselves, he is old enough to speak for himself."

Then the Pharisees again called the man who had been born blind and they said to him, "Give God the praise. We know that this man who made you to see is a sinner." He said to them, "I do not know whether or not he is a sinner. One thing I do know is that I was blind, but now I see." The Pharisees said, "What did he do to you? How did he open your eyes?" The man said, "I have already told you, and you did not hear. If

I tell it to you again, then will you also be his disciples?" Then they insulted the man and said, "You are his disciple, but we are Moses' disciples. We know that God spoke to Moses, but as for this fellow, we do not know where he came from." The man said to them, "Herein is a marvelous thing: you do not know where he came from and yet he opened my eyes. Now, we know that God does not hear sinners, but God hears those who worship Him and do His will. Since the beginning of the world, has anyone opened the eyes of someone who was born blind? If this man were not of God, he could do nothing." The Pharisees said to him, "You were born in sin, and you dare to preach to us!" And they threw him out.

Jesus heard that the Pharisees had ostracized the former blind man and he went to find him. When he had found him Jesus asked the man, *"Do you believe on the Son of God?"* The man answered, "Who is he, Lord, so that I might believe on him?" Jesus said to him, *"You have both seen him, and it is He that speaks with you."* The man said, "Lord, I believe!" Then the man began to worship Jesus. Jesus said, *"For judgment I have come into the world, so that those who cannot see might be made to see and those who see might be made blind."* Some of the Pharisees, which were with the man, heard these words and said to Jesus, "Are we blind also?" Jesus said to them, *"If you were blind then you would have no sin, but because you say, 'we see', therefore your sin remains."*

The Pharisees And Sadducees Try To Trap Jesus

One day the Sadducees came to Jesus and, not believing in the resurrection, they said to him, "Master, Moses said that if a man dies before having any children then his brother should marry the man's wife and raise his seed with her for his brother. Now, there were seven brothers. The first, after he was married, died leaving no children. The second brother married the first brother's wife, but he also died before having any children with her. Likewise, the third, fourth and fifth brothers, all the way to the seventh brother died without having children with the woman. Last of all, the woman died also. Therefore, in the resurrection, whose wife will she be?"

Jesus answered them, "*You do not know the scriptures or the power of God. In the resurrection there will be neither marrying nor giving into marriage. They will be like the angels in heaven. In speaking about the resurrection, haven't you read, 'I am the God of Abraham, Isaac and Jacob'? Therefore, God is not the God of the dead, but of the living.*" Those people in the multitude who heard this were astonished.

Jesus asked the Sadducees, "*What do you think of the Messiah, whose son is he?*" They answered, "He is the son of David." Jesus said to them, "*How is it that David called him Lord saying, 'The Lord said unto my Lord, "Sit at my right hand until I make your enemies into your footstool"?' If David called him 'Lord' then how is He his son?*" No one was able to answer Jesus, and they became speechless concerning him.

When the Pharisees heard that Jesus had silenced the Sadducees they took council together. One of them asked Jesus, "Master, which is the greatest commandment in the Law?" Jesus answered, "*You shall love God with all your heart, and with all your mind and with all your soul. This is the first and greatest commandment.*

And the second greatest commandment is like it.

The Gospel of Jesus the Christ

You shall love your neighbor as yourself. On these two
commandments hang all the Law and the prophets."

The Parable Of The Good Samaritan

One of the Pharisees asked Jesus, "Who is
my neighbor?" Jesus answered him and said, "*A*
certain man went down from Jerusalem to Jericho and
fell among thieves. They stripped him of his clothing,
then beat and robbed him, leaving the man half dead.
By chance a certain priest came along that same
road, and when he saw the man he passed by on the
other side of the road. Likewise, a Levite, when he saw
the man, passed by on the other side of the road.
A certain Samaritan, as he journeyed, came upon
the man and had compassion on him. He went to him
and bound his wounds. He set him on his horse and
brought him to an inn, and he took care of him. In the
morning, when he was leaving, the Samaritan took out
two pence and he gave them to the innkeeper saying,
'Take care of him. And if you spend more than this,
then when I come back this way again I will repay you
whatever I owe.'
Now, which of the three was a neighbor toward the
man who fell among the thieves?"

The Pharisee said, "The one who showed mercy on him." Jesus said, *"You, also, go and do likewise."*

Jesus Condemns The Pharisees And Sadducees

Jesus spoke to the multitude and to his disciples saying, *"The Pharisees and Sadducees sit in the seat of Moses. Therefore, you should observe whatever they tell you, but do not be like them because they say one thing and do another.*

They bind heavy burdens and put them on people's shoulders, and they will not lift one finger to remove them. Everything they do is to be seen by others.

They make their phylacteries wide and their tassels long, and they love to sit in the uppermost room at feasts and in the chief seats in the synagogues. They love to be greeted in the marketplace and to be called 'Rabbi.' But you will not be called 'Rabbi' because there is only one who is your Master, and that one is the Christ. And the one who is the greatest among you will be your servant. Whoever exalts himself will be humbled and whoever humbles himself will be exalted.

Woe to you, Pharisees and elders of the law! You hypocrites! You shut the door to the kingdom of heaven against people. You never enter in and you prevent others from entering.

Woe to you, Pharisees and elders of the law! You hypocrites! You devour widows' houses and make long prayers for a pretense. Therefore, you will receive the greater damnation.

Woe to you, Pharisees and elders of the law! You hypocrites! You travel over land and sea to find one convert, and when you find him you make him twice the child of hell that you are!

Woe to you, blind guides. You say, 'Whoever swears by the temple, it is nothing. But whoever swears by the gold in the temple is a debtor.' You fools! Which is greater, the gold in the temple or that which sanctifies the gold in the temple?

You say, 'Whoever swears by the altar, it is nothing. But whoever swears by the gift on the altar is guilty.' You fools! Which is greater, the gift or the altar that sanctifies the gift?

Therefore, whoever swears by the altar swears by it and everything on it. And whoever swears by the temple swears by it and everything in it. And whoever swears by heaven swears by the throne of God and the One who sits on it.

Woe to you, Pharisees and elders of the law! You hypocrites! You pay tithes of mint, anise and cumin

*but ignore the more important matters of the Law;
mercy and faith. These you should have done and not
left the others undone. You blind guides! You strain at
a gnat and swallow a camel.*

*Woe to you, Pharisees and elders of the law!
You clean the outside of the cup and platter, while
the inside is full of extortion and excesses. You blind
guides! First cleanse that which is inside so that the
outside will be clean also.*

*Woe to you, Pharisees and elders of the law! You
hypocrites! You are like white sepulchers that outwardly appear beautiful, but are filled with dead mens'
bones within. Even as you also outwardly appear
righteous to others, but within are full of hypocrisy
and iniquities.*

*Woe to you, Pharisees and elders of the law! You
hypocrites! You build the tombs of the prophets and
garnish the sepulchers of the righteous and you say, 'If
we had been here in the days of our fathers, we would
not have partaken in the spilling of the blood of the
prophets.' Therefore, you are witnesses of yourselves
as being the children of those who killed the prophets.
Fill up with the measure of your fathers! You are the
generation of vipers! How can you escape the damnation of hell?*

The Gospel of Jesus the Christ

*Therefore, I send to you prophets, wise men and
scribes. Some of them you will kill and crucify, and
some you will scourge in your synagogues. You will
persecute them from city to city, and upon you will
come all the righteous blood that has been spilled
upon the earth, from the blood of righteous Abel to
the blood of righteous Zachariah, whom you killed
between the temple and the altar.*

*O Jerusalem, Jerusalem! You, who kill the prophets
and stone those who are sent to you by God. How often I have wished to gather your children together, as a
mother hen gathers her chicks under her wings, but you
would not let me!*

*Behold, your house is left to you desolate. I say
to you that you will not see me again until you say,
'Blessed is the One that comes in the name of God!'* "

The Signs Of The End Of The World

Jesus left the temple and his disciples came
to him, showing him the buildings of the temple.
Jesus said, *"Do you see all these buildings? Verily I say
to you that there will not be one stone here that is not
thrown to the ground."*

As Jesus sat on the Mount of Olives, his

disciples came to him privately, saying, "Tell us when these things will happen. What will be the signs to watch for with your coming and the signs of the end of the world?"

Jesus answered and said to them, *"Be careful that no one deceives you. Many will come in my name and say 'I am the Christ' and will deceive many people.*

You will hear of wars and rumors of wars, but do not worry. All of these things must come to pass, but the end is not yet. Nation will rise against nation, and kingdom against kingdom. There will be famines and pestilences, and earthquakes in various places. All these things are the beginning of sorrows.

You will be delivered up to the courts to be tortured and killed, and you will be hated by all nations because of me. Many people will be offended because of me and will betray each other.

Many false prophets will rise and deceive many people, and the love of many will grow cold, but those who endure to the end will be saved. This gospel will be preached throughout the whole world as a witness to all nations, and then the end will come.

Therefore, when you see the 'abomination of desolation,' which was spoken of by the prophet

*Daniel, standing in the Holy Place, then those who
are in Judea flee to the mountains! No one on the
housetops should go down to take anything from
his house nor should anyone in the field go back
for his clothes.*

*Woe to the pregnant women and nursing mothers
in those days! Pray that your flight does not take place
during the winter or on the Sabbath day, for there will
be a great tribulation, such as never has been seen before and never will be seen again. No one would be
saved if those days were not shortened, but for the sake
of the Elect those days will be shortened.*

*Then, at that time, if anyone says, 'Look, there is
the Christ!' do not believe it. False Christs and false
prophets will appear and will perform many great signs
and wonders, and will deceive many people. If they say
to you, 'He is in the desert' do not go, or 'He is in the
secret chamber' do not believe it. As the lightning
comes from the east and is visible even in the west,
so likewise will be the coming of the Son of Man.*

*Immediately after the tribulation in those days, the
sun will be darkened and the moon will no longer give
her light. The stars will fall from the heavens and the
powers in the heavens will be shaken. Then the sign of
the Son of Man will appear in the sky and all of the*

nations of the earth will mourn, and they will see the Son of Man coming on the clouds of heaven with power and great glory.

He will send forth his angels with the sound of a great trumpet and they will gather together the Elect from the four winds, from one end of the heavens and the earth to another.

Now, learn from the parable of the fig tree, 'when the branch is still tender and begins to grow leaves, you know that summer is near.' So likewise, when you see all of these things happening you will know that the time is near, even at the door.

I say to you that this generation will not pass away until all of these things have been fulfilled. Heaven and earth will pass away, but my Words will never pass away.

Not even the angels in heaven know what day or what hour that time will be, but only God. As in the days of Noah, the people were eating and drinking, marrying and giving in marriage before the flood until Noah entered the ark, so likewise will be the coming of the Son of Man. Two men will be in the field; one will be taken and the other left. Two women will be grinding at the mill; one will be taken and the other left.

Therefore, be watchful, because you do not know

when your Lord will come. Know that if the owner of the house had known when the thief was coming, he would have watched at that time and his house would not have been broken into. Therefore, you should always be ready.

Who is a faithful and wise servant, whose master has made him ruler over his household to give the other servants their meals at the proper times? Blessed is that servant, if the master finds him doing so when he returns. Then the master will make him ruler over all his possessions. But if that servant says to himself 'my master delays his return' and begins to beat his fellow servants and to eat and drink with drunkards, then the master of that servant will come on a day when the servant is not expecting him. The master will cut him down and appoint him a place with the hypocrites, where there will be weeping and gnashing of teeth. And that servant, who knew his Lord's will but did not do it, will be beaten with many lashes. But those that did not know, and did commit things worthy of stripes, will be beaten with few lashes. For unto those to whom much is given much will be required, and to those to whom people have committed much, of them they will ask the most.

The Kingdom of God is like ten virgins who took

their lamps and went to meet their bridegroom. Five
of them were foolish and five of them were wise. The
foolish ones took their lamps, but did not take any
extra oil for the lamps with them. The wise ones took
extra oil for their lamps.

The bridegroom was a very long time in coming,
and the virgins became drowsy and fell asleep. About
the twelfth hour there was a great cry, 'The bridegroom
is coming! Let's go out to meet him!' Then all the virgins got up and trimmed their lamps.

The foolish said to the wise, 'Give us some of
your oil, because our lamps have gone out!' The wise
answered, 'We cannot. There might not be enough for
all of us. Go to the market and buy some more oil for
yourselves.'

While they went to buy the oil the bridegroom
came and those who were ready for him went into
the wedding and the door was closed. Later, the other
virgins came and tried to enter the wedding, saying,
'Lord, Lord! Let us in!' The bridegroom answered, 'I
do not know you.'

Therefore, watch and be ready, because you do
not know the day or the hour when the Son of Man
will return.

The kingdom of heaven is like a man traveling into

a far country. He called his servants to him and turned over his land and possessions to them. He gave one of them five talents, to another he gave two talents and to the other he gave one talent. He gave to each according to his abilities, and then he began his long journey.

The servant who received the five talents went out and traded them for five more talents, besides the five he already had. Likewise, the servant who had received two talents went out and made another two. But the man who had the one talent went and dug a hole and buried the talent.

After a very long time the master of the house returned and went to settle accounts with his servants. The one who had received the five talents came and brought the other five talents, saying, 'Master, you gave me five talents and I have gained five more.' The master of the house said, 'Well done, good and faithful servant! You have been faithful with a few things, so I will make you ruler over many things. Go into the house of your Lord with joy!'

Then the servant who had been given two talents came and said, 'Master, I also have turned the two talents into two more.' The master of the house said, 'Well done, good and faithful servant! You have been faithful with a few things, so I will make you ruler over many things. Go into the house of your Lord with joy!'

Then the servant who had received the one talent came and said, 'Master, I know that you are a hard man, reaping where you have not sown and gathering where you have not scattered. I was afraid, and I hid your talent in the ground. Here is the one talent that you gave to me.'

The master of the house said, 'You wicked and lazy servant! You know that I reap where I have not sown and gather where I have not scattered. Therefore, you should have put my money in a bank. At least then I would have received interest on it. Give the one talent that you have there and give it to the servant with ten talents. Everyone who has will be given more, and he will have in abundance. Whoever does not have, even that which he has will be taken from him.'

Then the master of the house commanded his other servants, saying, 'Take the unprofitable servant and throw him outside, into the darkness, where there will be weeping and gnashing of teeth.' "

Then Jesus spoke another parable to them, saying, "There was a certain judge in a city who neither feared God nor regarded man. And there was a certain widow in that city who came to him saying, 'Avenge me of my adversary.' He would not for a *while, but afterwards he relented. Listen to what the corrupt judge said: 'Though I neither fear God nor respect men, yet because this widow troubles me, I will give her justice, for fear that by her continual pleading she wearies me.' And shall not God avenge His own Elect, which cry day and night to Him? I tell you that He will avenge them speedily. Nevertheless, when the Son of Man comes, will he find faith on the earth?*

When the Son of Man comes with his angels in all his glory, he will gather all the nations of the earth before him and he will separate them, as a shepherd divides the sheep from the goats. He will set the sheep on his right hand and the goats on the left.

The King will say to those on his right hand, 'Come, you who are blessed by God, and inherit the kingdom prepared for you since the foundation of the world! I was hungry and you gave me something to eat. I was thirsty and you gave me something to drink. I was a stranger and you took me in. I was naked and you gave me clothes. I was sick and you cared for me. I was in prison and you came to visit me.'

The righteous will answer him, 'Lord, when did we see you hungry and feed you? Or thirsty and give you something to drink? When did we see you as a stranger and take you in? Or naked and clothe you? When did we see you sick and care for you? Or in prison and visited you?'

The King will answer them, 'Inasmuch as you have done it for one of the very least of my brothers or sisters, you have done it for me.'

Then he will say to those on his left, 'Depart from me, evildoers, into the everlasting fire prepared for the devil and his angels. For I was hungry and you did not give me anything to eat. I was thirsty and you did not give me anything to drink. I was a stranger and you did not take me in. I was naked and you did not clothe me. I was sick and you did not care for me. I was in prison and you did not visit me.'

They will say to him, 'Lord, when did we see you hungry, or thirsty, or a stranger, or naked, or sick, or in prison and did not minister to you?'

He will answer them, 'I say to you, inasmuch as you did not do it for one of the very least of my brothers or sisters you did not do it for me.'

And those on the left will go into everlasting punishment, but those on the right will go into eternal life."

After Jesus had finished speaking these things he said to his disciples, "You know that the feast of the Passover is in two days, and the Son of Man will *be betrayed to be crucified.”*

Now, the chief priests and the scribes and the elders of the people assembled together in the palace of the high priest. They consulted each other about how they might kill Jesus. They said, “Not on the feast day because there will be an uproar among the people.”

Jesus Washes His Disciple's Feet

When Jesus was in Bethany, at the house of Simon the leper, a woman came to him carrying an alabaster box of very precious perfume. She poured the perfume on Jesus' head while he was eating dinner.

When the disciples saw this they became indignant and said, “What is this waste? This perfume could have been sold for a very high price, and the money given to the poor.”

When Jesus heard this he said, *“Leave the woman alone! She has done a very kind thing for me. You will always have the poor with you, but I will be with you for only a short time. In pouring this perfume on my body she is preparing me for burial. Verily I say to you that wherever this gospel is preached throughout the whole world, what this woman has done for me will also be preached in memory of her."*

Then one of the disciples, Judas Iscariot, went to the chief priests. He asked them, "What will you give me to deliver him to you?" They agreed to give Judas thirty pieces of silver. From that time on Judas sought an opportunity to betray Jesus.

Before the feast of the Passover, when Jesus and his disciples had finished eating dinner, he laid aside his garments, took a towel and girded himself. He poured water into a basin and began to wash the disciple's feet, and to wipe them with the towel that girded him. Then Jesus came to Peter and Peter asked him, "Lord, do you intend to wash my feet also?" Jesus answered, *"You do not realize what I do now, but after you will understand."* Peter said to him, "You will never wash my feet." Jesus said, *"If I don't wash you, then you have no part with me."* Peter said to him, "Lord, wash not only my feet, but also my hands and my head!" Jesus said, *"Those that are washed are every bit clean, but not every one of you is clean."* Jesus knew who would betray him; therefore he said, *"Not every one of you is clean."*

The Gospel of Jesus the Christ

After Jesus had finished washing his disciple's feet, he put his garments back on, sat down again and said to them, *"Do you know what I have done to you? You call me Master and Lord, and so I am. If I, your Lord and Master, have washed your feet, then you also should wash one another's feet. For I have given you an example that you should do to each other as I have done to you. Verily, verily, I say to you that the servant is not greater than his Lord. Neither is He that is sent greater than the One that sent him. If you know these things, then you will be happy if you do them."*

Jesus Is Betrayed And Is Crucified

On the first day of the Passover the disciples came to Jesus, saying, "Where will we eat during the Passover?" Jesus said, *"Go into the city to a certain man and tell him that your Master says, 'My appointed time is near. I will keep the Passover at your house with my disciples.'"* The disciples did as they were instructed and prepared for the feast of the Passover.

When evening came Jesus sat down with the twelve disciples. As they were eating he said,

"*Verily, I say to you that one of you will betray me.*" They were very sad and each disciple began to ask, "Lord, is it I?"

Jesus answered and said, "*The one who dips his hand with me in the dish, the same one will betray me. The Son of Man will go as it has been written, but woe to the man who betrays him! It would be better if that man had never been born.*"

Then Judas asked Jesus, "Lord, is it I?" Jesus said, "*It is as you say it is.*"

While they were eating Jesus took his bread and broke it saying, "*Take it and eat, as this is my body.*" He took the cup and, after giving thanks, he gave it to his disciples, saying, "*Drink all of it, as this is my blood of the New Testament, which is shed for many for the remission of sins.*"

When they had finished eating they went to the Mount of Olives and Jesus said to them, "*Little children, I am with you for only a little while longer. You will look for me, and as I said to the Pharisees, you will not find me. I now give to you a new commandment, and that is that you shall love one another as I have loved you. And by this shall all people know that you are my disciples; that you love one another.*

The Gospel of Jesus the Christ

There is no greater love anyone can have than to lay down his life for his friends. You are my friends, if you do what I have commanded of you. You have not chosen me but I have chosen you, so that you shall go and bring forth fruit, and your fruit shall remain.

From now on I will not call you servants, because the servant does not know what his lord does. I have called you friends, because all things that I have heard from my Father I have revealed to you.

If the world hates you, then you will know that it hated me before you. If you were of the world, then the world would love you. But because you are not of the world because I have chosen you out of the world, therefore the world hates you.

Remember the Words that I have spoken to you. The servant is not greater than his lord. If they have persecuted me, then they will also persecute you. If they have kept my sayings, then they will keep yours also.

These things I have spoken to you so that you will not be offended. They will put you out of the synagogues, and the time is coming when those who kill you will think they are doing God's work. These things they will do because they have not known God, nor me.

The Gospel of Jesus the Christ

I have told you these things ahead of time, and be-cause I have told you these things your hearts are filled with sorrow.

Verily, verily, I say to you that unless a kernel of wheat falls into the ground and dies it will abide alone, but if it dies it will bring forth much fruit.

Nevertheless, I tell you the truth. It is expedient for you that I go away, because if I do not go away the Comforter will not come to you. When I depart I will send him to you. When he comes he will reprove the world of sin and of righteousness, and of judgment.

Of sin, because they believed not on me;

Of righteousness, because I go to my Father;

Of judgment, because the prince of this world is judged.

A little while, and you shall not see me again.

A little while, and you shall see me again because I go to my Father."

Then some of the disciples said among them-selves, "What is he saying to us, *'a little while and we shall not see him, and a little while and we shall see him'?* We do not understand what he is saying."

Jesus knew that his disciples desired to ask him and he said, *"Do you inquire among yourselves of what I said, 'A little while and you shall not see me, and a little while and you shall see me'?*

Verily, verily, I say to you that you shall weep and lament, but the world will rejoice. You shall be sorrowful, but your sorrow will be turned into joy.

A woman, when she is in labor, has sorrow. But as soon as she has delivered the baby she no longer remembers the anguish. Instead there is joy that a child is born into the world. You are now sorrowful, but I will see you again and then your sorrow will be turned into joy.

I have told you these things so that you may find peace through me. You will have tribulation in this world, but be of good cheer because I have overcome the world.

Where I go, you cannot follow me now. But you will follow me afterwards.

Tonight all of you will be offended because of me, for it is written, 'I will strike the shepherd and the sheep will be scattered abroad.' But after I have risen, I will go ahead of you to Galilee."

Then Peter said to Jesus, "Lord, though all men will be offended because of you, I will never be offended." Jesus said to him, *"I tell you that before this night is over, before the rooster crows, you will* deny me three times.

Let not your hearts be troubled, neither let them be afraid. In my Father's house there are many mansions. If it were not so, I would have told you. I go to prepare a place for you. And if I go and prepare a place for you, I will come again and bring you to me. Wherever I am, there you may be also. You know where I am going, and you know the way."

Thomas said, "Lord, We do not know where you are going, how are we suppose to know the way?" Jesus said to him, *"I am the Way, the Truth and the Life. No one comes to my Father, except by me. If you know me, then you know my Father also. Henceforth you know him and have seen him."*

Philip said to Jesus, "Lord, show us the Father." Jesus said to him, *"How long have I been with you, Philip, and you still do not know me? The one who has seen me has seen my Father. How then can you say, 'Show us the Father'? Do you not believe that I am in the Father, and the Father is in me? The Words that I speak are not mine, but the Father that dwells in me speaks through me, and he does the works. Believe me when I say that I am in the Father and the Father is in me, or else believe me for the very works' sake.*

The Gospel of Jesus the Christ

Verily, verily, I say to you that the one who believes on me shall do the works that I do and even greater works than these, because I go into my Father. And whatever you ask in my name, that I will do, so that the Father may be glorified in the Son. If you ask anything in my name, I will do it for you.

If you love me, keep my commandments. And I will pray to God and he shall give you another Comforter, which will abide with you forever. God will give to you the Spirit of Truth, whom the world cannot receive because it neither sees nor knows him. But you know him, because he dwells in you.

I will not leave you comfortless. I will come to you. The Comforter, which is the Holy Spirit, whom God will send in my name, will teach you all things, and will help you remember everything I have taught you.

Yet in a little while the world will not see me, but you will see me. And because I live, you also will live. On that day you will know that I am in my Father and you are in me, and I am in you.

Whoever knows and keeps my commandments loves me. God will love whoever loves me and I will love him, and I will show myself to him."

Then one of the disciples asked Jesus, "Lord, how can you show yourself to us and not to the world?" Jesus answered and said to him, "*If anyone loves me he will keep my teachings, and my Father will love him. We will come to him, and make our abode with him. I am the true vine and God is the husbandman. Every branch in me that does not bear fruit is taken away, and every branch that bears fruit is purged, so that it may bring forth more fruit. Now you are clean through the Word, which I have spoken to you. Abide in me, and I will abide in you. As the branch cannot bear fruit of itself unless it abides in the vine, so likewise you cannot bear fruit unless you abide in me. I am the vine and you are the branches. The one who abides in me and I in him brings forth much fruit, for without me you can do nothing. Herein is God glorified; that you bear much fruit, and therefore you will be known as my disciples.*

As God has loved me, so have I loved you. Continue all of you in my love. If you keep my teachings you shall abide in my love, even as I have kept God's commandments and abide in his love.

These things I have spoken to you so that my joy might remain in you, and so that your joy might be made full."

Then Jesus lifted up his eyes to heaven and said, "*Father, the hour is come. Glorify your Son, so that your Son may glorify you. You have given him power over all flesh, so that he can give eternal life to as many people as you have given to him.*

I have glorified you to the world, and I have finished the work that you gave me to do. I have manifested your name to those whom you gave to me and they have kept your Word.

I have given them the Word that you gave to me and they have received the Word. They have surely known that I came from you and they have believed that you sent me. All of mine are yours and yours are mine, and I am glorified through them.

And now I am no longer in the world, but these are in the world. God, please keep through your own name those whom you have given to me, so that they may be as One even as we are One.

I not only pray for these alone, but also for those who will believe on me through their words; that they all may be as One. Even as you are in me and I am in you; let them also be One in us, so that the love with which you have loved me may also be in them."

Jesus and the disciples came to a place called Gethsemane and Jesus said to them, "*Sit down here while I go over there and pray.*"

Jesus took Peter and the two sons of Zebedee

with him. Jesus said to them, "*My heart is filled with sorrow, even unto death. Wait here and watch with me.*"

Then Jesus went ahead a little further and fell on his face and began to pray, saying, "*Father, if it is possible, let this cup pass from me. Even so God, your will, not mine, be done.*"

When Jesus returned to the disciples he found them asleep. Jesus said to Peter, "*You could not watch with me for just one hour? Watch and pray, so that you do not fall into temptation. The Spirit is willing, but the flesh is weak.*"

He went away again the second time and prayed, saying, "*God, if this cup may not pass from me, except that I drink it, then your will be done.*" Jesus came and found the disciples asleep again and he said to them, "*Sleep on now, and take your rest. The hour is at hand, and the Son of Man is betrayed into the hands of sinners.*"

While Jesus was still speaking, a great mob came led by Judas. Judas had told the chief priest, "Whomever I kiss, that one is Jesus."

He went up to Jesus and drew near to kiss him. Jesus said to him, "*Judas, you betray me with a kiss?*"

Then the officers of the high priest came and arrested Jesus. One of the disciples drew a sword and struck an officer of the high priest, cutting off his ear. Jesus said to him, *"Put away the sword. Those who live by the sword will die by the sword. Do you think that I cannot pray to my Father, and he will send twelve legions of angels? How then will the scriptures be fulfilled which say that it must be this way?"*

Jesus said to the multitude that had come to arrest him, *"Have you come out as against a thief with swords and staves to take me? I sat daily with you teaching in the temple, and you laid no hold on me. All this was done so that the scriptures of the prophets might be fulfilled."* Then all the disciples abandoned Jesus and ran.

The ones who had arrested Jesus took him to Caiaphas, the high priest. The scribes and elders of the law were assembled there also.

Peter followed them from a distance to the high priest's palace and went in and sat with the servants to see the result of the meeting.

The chief priest and elders of the law looked for witnesses against Jesus so that they could have him put to death. Many people came forward, but none would lie in order to convict him.

Finally, two people came and said, "This fellow said, 'I am able to destroy the temple of God and rebuild it in three days.' "

The high priest asked Jesus, "Are you going to answer to these charges?" But Jesus would not reply.

The high priest said to him, "I ask you in the name of the living God, are you the Christ, the Son of God?"

Jesus answered them, saying, *"It is as you say. Nevertheless, I say to you that you will see the Son of Man sitting on the right hand of God, and coming on the clouds of heaven."*

The high priest said, "He has spoken blasphemy! What further proof do we need? You heard his blasphemy! What do you think?" The elders of the law answered, "He is guilty and should be put to death."

They spit in Jesus' face and hit him repeatedly. Others struck him with the palms of their hands, saying, "Prophesy to us, Christ. Who hit you?"

As Peter sat outside, a woman came to him and said, "You were with Jesus of Galilee." Peter denied this in front of all of them, saying,

"I don't know what you're talking about."

He went onto the porch and another woman saw him and said to everyone there, "This man was also with Jesus of Nazareth." Peter again denied knowing Jesus. He said with an oath, "I do not know the man."

After awhile those who were standing there came to Peter and said, "Surely you are one of them. Your accent gives you away." Peter began to curse and to swear, saying, "I do not know the man!" Immediately a rooster crowed and Peter remembered the words of Jesus, *"Before the rooster crows, you will deny me three times."* Then Peter went out and wept bitterly.

The chief priest and elders of the law took council together the next morning and tried to have Jesus put to death. They tied him up and led him away. Then they delivered him to Pontius Pilate, the governor.

When Judas, who had betrayed Jesus, saw that Jesus had been sentenced to die, he repented and went back to the chief priest, and brought with him the thirty pieces of silver. He said to the chief priest and elders of the law, "I have sinned because I have betrayed innocent blood."

The chief priest replied to him, "What is that to us? You, yourself, will have to answer to that." Judas threw down the thirty pieces of silver and left. Then he went out and hanged himself.

The chief priest took the silver pieces and said, "It is not lawful for us to keep this because it is blood money." So they took the silver and bought the potter's field, which is a place to bury strangers. That is why it is known to this very day as 'the field of blood.'

Therefore, it was fulfilled what was spoken by the prophet Jeremy, "They took the thirty pieces of silver, the price of the one who was valued by the children of Israel, and they gave them for the potter's field."

When Jesus stood in front of the governor, and the governor asked him, "Are you the King of the Jews?" Jesus answered, *"Yes, it is as you say."* When the chief priests and elders of the law accused Jesus he would not reply.

Pilate went out again to the Jews and said to them, "I find no fault at all in this man. You have a custom at the Passover, that I release one prisoner to you. Would you like me to release to you the King of the Jews?" They cried out, "Not

this man, but Barabbas." Now, Barabbas was
a notorious criminal, being a murderer.

Pilate asked them, "What shall I do with
Jesus, who is called Christ?" They all said, "Crucify him." Pilate asked them, "Why? What crime
has he committed?" But they cried out even loud-
er, "Crucify him!"

So Pilate, wanting to appease the crowd,
delivered Jesus up to be crucified. The soldiers
led him away into the hall and they clothed him
with a purple robe and they platted a crown of
thorns and put it on his head. Then they began
to salute him and said, "Hail, King of the Jews!"

They struck Jesus on the head with a stick and
spit on him. Then they got on their knees as if to
worship him. After they had finished mocking
him, they removed the purple robe and put his
own clothes back on him, and led him out to be
crucified.

They brought him to a place called Golgatha
and they gave him wine mixed with gall, which
he did not drink. When they nailed him to the
cross they took his clothes, and each man took
whatever he wanted from them.

The superscription above Jesus' cross read:

'The King of the Jews.'

They crucified two thieves with him, one on the right and another on the left. Thus the prophecy was fulfilled, "He will be numbered among the transgressors."

When the sixth hour came there was darkness across the whole land until the ninth hour, and at the ninth hour Jesus cried out in a loud voice, *"My God, My God, why have you forsaken me?"* And then he gave up the ghost.

As soon as Jesus died there was a violent earthquake and the curtain in the temple was torn in half, from the very top to the very bottom. When the soldier who was guarding Jesus heard and saw these things he said, "Surely, this was the Son of God!"

As was the custom for the preparation of the Sabbath, no bodies were to be left on the cross. To ensure that those being crucified were dead, the soldiers broke their legs to hasten their deaths so that they might be taken away. The soldiers came and broke the legs of the first, and of the other that was crucified with him. But when they came to Jesus and saw that he was dead already, they did not break his legs.

The Gospel of Jesus the Christ

One of the soldiers took a spear and pierced his side, and at once blood and water poured out of the wound. Thus the scriptures were fulfilled: "a bone of Him shall not be broken" and "they shall look upon Him whom they pierced."

Joseph of Arimathea brought fine linen and, taking Jesus down from the cross, he wrapped the linen around Jesus' body and and laid him in a tomb made out of a rock. Mary Magdalene, who was a disciple of Jesus and Mary, the mother of James, saw where Jesus was laid.

The next day the chief priests and Pharisees went to Pilate. They said, "Sir, we remember that the imposter said, while he was still alive, *'After three days I will rise again.'* Therefore, command that the sepulcher be made secure until the third day, so his disciples don't come and steal him away and say to the people, 'He is risen from the dead', making the last error worse than the first."

Pilate said to them, "You have a guard. Go and make it as secure as you can." So they went and made the tomb secure, sealing the stone, and setting a watch.

The Gospel of Jesus the Christ

Jesus Is Risen From The Dead

On the day after the Sabbath, which was the third day after Jesus died, both Mary Magdalene and Mary, the mother of James, went to the tomb to anoint Jesus. When they arrived at the tomb there was a great earthquake and an angel of the Lord descended from heaven, and came and rolled back the stone from the door and sat upon it. His countenance was like lightning, and his clothing white as snow. And for fear of him, the guards shook and became as dead men.

The angel said to the women, "Do not be afraid. Jesus of Nazareth, whom you are seeking, has arisen. Go and tell his disciples to meet him in Galilee, and there they will find him." They departed quickly with fear and great joy, and ran to bring the disciples the message. As they were going to deliver the message to the disciples, Jesus met them saying, *"Hello!"* They came and held him by the feet, and worshiped him. Then Jesus said to them, *"Do not be afraid. Go and tell my brothers to go to Galilee, and there they will see me."*

Now, after they had left, some of the guards

went into the city and told the chiefs priests what had happened. The chief priests took counsel with the elders and together they gave large sums of money to the guards and told them, "Say that his disciples came by at night, while you were sleeping, and stole him away. And if the governor hears about this, we will protect you." So they took the money and did as they were instructed, and this version is commonly reported among the Jewish people to this day.

The Final Commission

Now, when the disciples heard that Jesus was alive and had been seen by the women, they did not believe it.

Afterwards Jesus appeared in another form to two of the disciples as they were walking in the country. And they went and told it to the remaining disciples, but they did not believe them.

Then Jesus appeared to the disciples as they were eating supper and he scolded them for not believing those whom had seen him after he was risen. The disciples were frightened and assumed that they were seeing a ghost. Jesus said to them,

The Gospel of Jesus the Christ

"Why are you troubled? And why do these thoughts arise in your hearts? Look at my hands and my feet! Touch me and you will believe. Does a ghost have flesh and bones?" When Jesus had spoken these words, he showed the disciples his hands and his feet. Then the disciples were filled with joy. Jesus said, *"Do you have anything here to eat?"* They gave him a piece of a broiled fish and a honeycomb. And Jesus did eat in front of the disciples. Afterward, Jesus vanished from their sight.

Thomas, one of the twelve, was not with them when Jesus came. The other disciples said to him, "We have seen the Lord." Thomas said, "Unless I see the holes of the nails in his hands and put my finger in them, and thrust my hand into his side, I will not believe."

After eight days the disciples were inside, and this time Thomas was with them. Jesus came and stood in the middle of them and said to Thomas, *"Put your fingers in the holes of my hands, and put your hand into my side. Don't be faithless, but believe."* Then Thomas began to worship Jesus and Jesus said, *"Thomas, because you have seen, you believe. Blessed are those that have not seen, and yet believe."*

This was now the third time Jesus showed

himself to his disciples after he was raised from the dead. So when they had dined, Jesus said to Simon Peter, *"Simon, son of Jonas, do you love me?"* Peter answered, "Yes, Lord, you know that I love you." Jesus said, *"Feed my sheep."* Then Jesus asked Peter again, *"Simon, son of Jonas, do you love me?"* Peter said, "Yes, Lord, you know that I love you." Jesus said, *"Feed my sheep."* Then Jesus asked Peter a third time, *"Simon, son of Jonas, do you love me?"* Peter was grieved because he had said to him a third time, *"Do you love me?"* Peter said to Jesus, "Lord, you know all things. You already know that I love you." Jesus said to him, *"Feed my sheep. Verily, verily, I say to you that when you were young, you clothed yourself and walked wherever you wanted to go, but when you are old another will clothe you and carry you where you do not want to go."* Jesus spoke this signifying by what death Peter would glorify God. And after speaking this Jesus said, *"Follow me."* Then Jesus opened their understanding, so that they could comprehend the scriptures.

Afterwards, Jesus led them out as far as Bethany and He said to them, *"All authority in heaven and on earth has been given to me. Go into every part of the world and preach the gospel to every living creature, teaching them to observe everything I have commanded of you. Those who believe and are baptized will be saved, but those who do not believe will be condemned. And behold, I am with you always, even to the very end of the world."* After Jesus had finished speaking to them, He lifted up his hands toward heaven and He blessed the disciples. And as He blessed them, He was parted from them and taken straightway up into the heavens to sit at the right hand of God.

Bibliography

This Bible was compiled and edited from these sources with appreciation and gratitude for these Great Bodhisattvas:

Goddard, Dwight, editor, 1861-1939,
A Buddhist Bible, Boston, Beacon Press, c1938, 1970.

Muller, F. Max, editor and translator, 1823-1900,
The Dhammapada, Oxford University Press, 1870.

H. Kern and Muller, F. Max, editors and translators, 1823-1900, *Saddharma Pundarika or The Lotus of the True Law,* Motilal Barnsidass Publishers (Sacred Books of the East), 1884.

Kato, Bunno and Soothill, William E., 1861-1935, editors and translators, *The Threefold Lotus Sutra,* New York/ Weatherhill, 1975.

T.W. and C.A.F. Rhys Davids, translators, 1843-1922, *Dialogues of the Buddha, volume 3; Chakkavatti Sihanada Suttanta,* Pali Text Society, 1921

Minayeff, Jeff, editor, *The Anagatavamsa,* Journal of the Pali Text Society, 1886.

The Gospels of Saints Matthew, Mark, Luke & John, *The Holy Bible* (King James Version), circa 1611 A.D.

LaVergne, TN USA
10 January 2010
169475LV00001B/1/P